The Red Dragon
and
The Rising Sun

PRELUDE

H. Noel Davies

Elwyn Thomas,

General view of Tylorstown

The Red Dragon and The Rising Sun
PRELUDE

Noel Davies

Illustrated by Elwyn Thomas

1987
D. BROWN AND SONS
COWBRIDGE · WALES

Dedicated to my wife
Mair

© 1987 Noel Davies

 ISBN 0 905928 62 8

The publishers wish to acknowledge the assistance of the Editorial Department of
the Welsh Books Council which is supported by the Welsh Arts Council.

DESIGNED AND PRINTED IN WALES BY
D. Brown and Sons Ltd., Cowbridge and Bridgend, Glamorgan

Contents

Illustrations

Foreword

In this book the author recalls his early memories and impressions of Tylorstown which is a typical Rhondda village and we share his boyhood recollections of New Quay, Dyfed, where he spent his summer holidays with his relatives.

We are also reminded of the sufferings of those who were unfortunate enough to become prisoners of war in the hands of the Japanese Imperial Army.

The book is expertly illustrated by Mr. Elwyn Thomas and his drawings enhance an interesting work. I have had the pleasure of knowing the author and the artist for many years and their combined efforts delight me. I wish the book every success!

Glyn James
Mayor of Rhondda 1985-6

Preface

The book is being produced in two Volumes. The first Volume can be regarded as a prelude to my captivity in the Far East, which lasted for three and a half years. It briefly covers family background in Rhondda, New Quay, Dyfed, and North Wales. Survival was partly due to inherited psychological and constitutional strengths handed down from generation to generation. It is hoped that with the help of the excellent illustrations which greatly enhance the work, this Volume will be well received so that the second Volume can be produced soon.

Acknowledgements

The Rev. W. Rhys Nicholas for his advice and help, and the Welsh Books Council for editing the manuscript. To my sister-in-law, Mrs. Olive Davies (Tonteg) and Mr. Alun Morgan (Porthcawl) for their invaluable help in the early stages. To the Industrial and Maritime Museum for information and to Mr. Elwyn Thomas for illustrating the work so excellently. Finally to Mair, my wife, for suggesting that I should undertake this work and finally to Mr. R. D. Whitaker of D. Brown and Sons Ltd., for producing the first Volume.

Introduction

A dderbyniasom, hynny a drosglwyddwn, o'n bodd neu'n hanfodd;
yr hyn a fu a wyddom—mewn dameg.

(What we have received, that we hand over, willing or unwilling;
What has been is what we know—in a tale.)*

I have sometimes asked myself if Christmas Day is the best of days on which to celebrate one's birthday. Certainly, it must have been a hectic Christmas Day in 1919 when I was born, at six o'clock in the morning, in Tylorstown in the Rhondda; the family already consisted of three children, their ages ranging from sixteen to eight years of age, so I must have been a complication in their lives from the moment they knew of my impending arrival.

Excited by the new arrival, my brother Ivor, only eight years old, but blessed with a natural spirit of enterprise, went, with excited determination, to spread the news to the other members of our family, as well as to a hastily-chosen selection of the more generous of our family friends. He had a twofold message: to wish them the compliments of the season, and to announce my arrival, and he was well rewarded for his efforts.

My sister, Elizabeth Morwen, was born in New Quay (now Dyfed, but then Cardiganshire). My mother had gone there to have her first baby in my grandparents' house in Rock Street, and her parents begged her to leave the baby with them. They wanted her to leave the grime and heavy industrialisation of the Rhondda Valley and return to New Quay, but this was not to be, and both my brothers were born in Church Terrace, Tylorstown.

Amidst all the upheaval of that eventful morning, good neighbours made sure that the Christmas dinner was cooked properly and my mother would tell me in years to come that this was the only Christmas when she failed to eat her dinner. She finally agreed some days later that I should be called Noel. However great the inconvenience caused by my birth, good neighbours said at the time that I would be lucky in life and looking back I cannot but conclude that this forecast was right.

*Pont y Caniedydd by Alun Llywelyn-Williams
from The Oxford Book of Welsh Verse in English chosen by Gwyn Jones

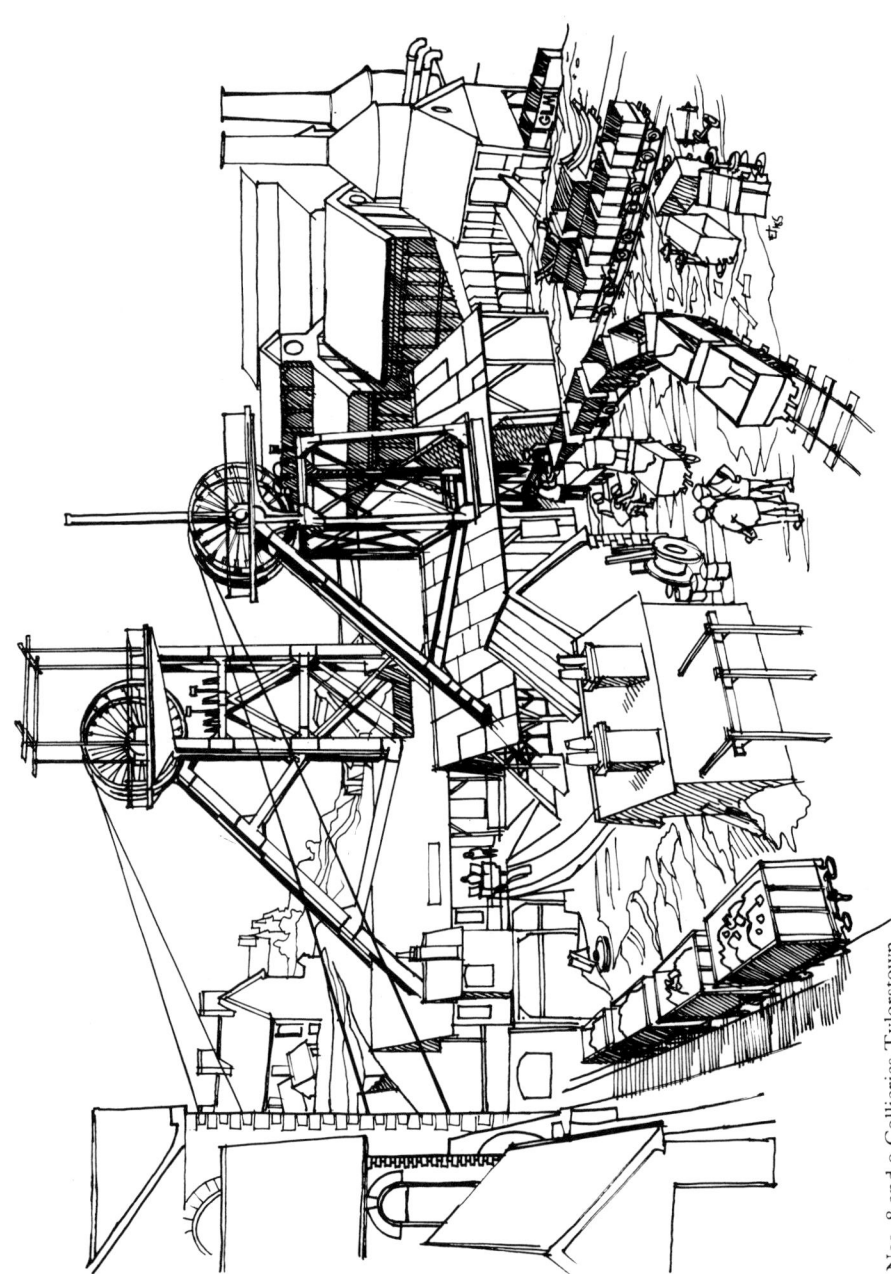

Nos. 8 and 9 Collieries Tylorstown.

Chapter 1

My father's family were from the northern part of Pembrokeshire, and he was born in a house called 'Parc y Llyn' near Letterston, not far from Fishguard, where my great grandparents were married, in Hermon Chapel. Welsh was the family's first language—many of the older members had only a smattering of English.

My father's father, David Davies, had been a farmer, but had not been successful, and even when given a second opportunity failed to make the farm pay. *His* father, James Davies, who had twice set him up in business, must have despaired of his son, who was next heard of in Tylorstown; family tradition portrays him as an irresponsible person who had a good start in life—unlike his son, my father, who had a poor start in life because of my grandfather's neglect, which destroyed family security before my father was born.

When David Davies worked in the Tylorstown collieries he was a 'haulier' and spent his time with horses and ponies. He would go to Ystrad Rhondda station when the animals arrived after experiencing travel in a cattle truck, which left them frightened, tired and very difficult to handle. Apparently he was able to calm them, not only by his manner but by talking to them in Welsh, the language they had been accustomed to on the farms where they had been reared.

The final calamity of his troubled life was his death in an explosion in one of the Tylorstown collieries. It took the rescue teams a week to bring his body to the surface, and my father remembers the older members of his family travelling to the funeral from Fishguard. After that my grandmother and her younger children lived in a small cottage between Fishguard and Letterston, and my father told me about the hard, even primitive, life they had as a family when they lived there. The cottage had a polished earth floor which softened in wet weather, so that the legs of the four-poster bed, the old dresser and the table sank into it; sometimes a rat would claw into the cottage through the soft earth floor. My father slept in a cupboard bed, a popular piece of furniture in Welsh country cottages, and said it was very cosy in winter-time.

My grandmother was ailing and food was scarce. The children took root crops from the edges of farmers' fields and once a week they waited for the cart laden with fresh fish from Fishguard and Goodwick.

As the cart passed their cottage they took a fish or two for the next meal, and thus lived from hand to mouth. Fortunately their mother sent them to school and chapel where they were taught important fundamentals. It was a hard life but they managed to survive on simple food and all the children lived to a ripe old age. My father was strong and active until he died at eighty-four years of age after an illness of a few days. He had never been ill in his long life and would have lived longer if he had allowed his children to help him. He retained his simplicity even though he had travelled the world and his actions often revealed that at one stage in his life he had been very poor.

My father's mother was Martha John, and although she was to suffer a difficult life and an early death, her childhood was happy and normal. She apparently was brought up on a farm which was run efficiently, and often spoke about her mother brewing beer and baking bread ready for the hired workers who came to gather in the harvest. My father helped in the fields at the end of the century, just before machinery replaced the scythes. A big cauldron of *cawl* would be prepared for the men and women, and my great grandmother was said to brew a good strong beer which was appreciated by the farm workers during the harvest.

My father went to a village school for a few years, where he learned to read Welsh and English and to do simple arithmetic, which enabled him to cope with everyday problems. His handwriting and spelling were more than satisfactory so that he was invited to accept responsibilities in chapel. He was able to address meetings in both languages and put forward his point of view so clearly that those who listened to him understood what he was telling them. When in the right mood he would talk of his childhood days, and was particularly interesting when telling of incidents in the little country school: one which evidently impressed him was when the schoolmaster unfortunately pushed the sharp end of a cricket stump into a boy's navel. The poor man used the cricket stump to keep the children at bay from his desk when he was marking their classwork. Fortunately no harm was done to the boy, but the calm of the little school was very disturbed that morning. Parents paid a penny per week for the education of each child. My father's brother, Harries, disliked school and spent his penny for most weeks. Consequently, he never learnt to read, which was very sad because he was a great personality and had an amazing memory. He was well-informed in current affairs and took part in many a family discussion—one would never know he was not a great reader.

My grandmother died at a very early age, of 'decline' (probably consumption), caused by a combination of worry, lack of food and security, poor living conditions and little or no medication. The children were consequently separated and, fortunately for them, placed in the care of relatives. My father was taken to the Drim Mill to his uncle and aunt, Henry and Naomi. The water mill was in Goodwick, down a hill from Fishguard, and half a mile from the sea.

My father's stay in the Drim Mill with Harry and Naomi, who were good, kindly people, was difficult at times because he was resentful rather than grateful, feeling that he was 'second class', a little better than an unpaid servant. He was made to carry heavy sacks of flour when he was fourteen years of age and Henry gave him the task of delivering them to the many farms in the district. For this purpose my father had a donkey and cart, travelling in every weather to reach their destination and deliver goods. In such awful conditions the donkey would become stubborn and refuse to budge, to the dismay and exasperation of my father. The animal would move only in his own time— indeed, in latter years my mother would maintain that the stubborn nature of the donkey had entered my father's personality!

This stubborness is, I'm afraid, a family characteristic, but in the face of difficulty can prove to be a helpful vice!

The view from Strumble Head in fine clear weather was a sight my father never tired of talking about and he loved the beauty and loneliness. In winter time, he returned in darkness which must have been frightening at times. Until new laws were passed, vehicles did not have sidelights and he remembered his uncle having to comply with the regulation. Travelling alone on dark evenings in those days had the added element of fear of meeting ghosts and demons. Age-old superstitions still gripped country people.

Life in rural Wales changed very little over the centuries and my father, being poor, was very aware of his absolute dependence on kindness and charity. He was respectful and accepted his lowly station in society, but a determination to improve his situation gradually developed. It is not easy for us to understand how poor people managed to survive when misfortune hit them.

According to my father, if he so wished he could have remained in the Fishguard area because he was needed in the Drim Mill. He enjoyed the hustle and bustle of Fishguard Square. The railway had not reached Fishguard, so a stage coach carrying mail arrived in Fishguard Square on certain days. It also brought passengers and their luggage into the town. One of my father's delights on Saturday morning was to wait for the coach and its fine team of horses to arrive. One morning, a deputation from Hermon Chapel was awaiting it, and on its arrival my father saw a famous man of the times alighting. It was the new minister, the Rev. Dan Davies, impressively dressed in a frock coat, a black travelling cloak and black silk top hat!—which accounted for the deputation of dignified deacons who were meeting him. Fishguard at this time had famous preachers, renowned throughout Wales and idolised in the same way as rugby and pop stars in modern times. They attracted large crowds; and when my father was a youth, he said that he stood in Fishguard Square on Sunday summer evenings and could hear the *hwyl* of preachers in different chapels as they brought their sermons to an end.

The old harbour was still the hub of commerce where sailing vessels arrived and sailed with their cargoes. There was no harbour in Goodwick and my father often helped to load and unload the ships at low tide as they lay at anchor. He would take the horse and cart to the side of the boat and the sea would be up to the cart's axle.

Some of the family eventually returned to Fishguard after some years in the Rhondda. My father's brother Ben, who had opened three barbers' shops in the mining valleys hired a traction engine to carry his furniture from Tylorstown to Fishguard. It took two days' slow travelling to complete the journey.

Ninety-year-old Naomi of the Drim Mill visited Tylorstown and stayed for a few days, so I went to see her. She was tall, slim and stately, despite her great age. She had lived sixty years of her life in the nineteenth century. The Industrial Revolution had not touched her part of the country, so she possessed the unruffled calm and assurance of a way of life that had prevailed unchanged for centuries. Karl Marx during his research for his *Das Kapital* had spent a considerable time in neighbouring Cardiganshire, around the time that Naomi was born, and had concluded that the workers of West Wales were a hundred years behind those who worked in the great English industrial towns as regards the way in which they were conscious of the strength of the working class if united in powerful unions. The agricultural workers of West Wales were more respectful of the authority wielded by those who had a better social status. They accepted their lowly position in society with little rancour or grumbling. Admittedly, there were riots in the countryside of West Wales because of the tolls collected on the turnpike roads, but this was to be put right, and the populace soon returned to its tranquil ways. Karl Marx produced the first *Communist Manifesto* in 1847 in which he urged the workers of industrialised Europe to unite themselves into powerful unions. I can't imagine my people being interested in these doctrines in the areas where they were living. Their society was tribal rather than feudal. There were powerful family loyalties, and Nonconformity derided wealth and rank. Poverty had to be overcome by hard work and thrift. My family accepted their place in society and were satisfied with trying to better their lot by their efforts.

My father, however, was determined to leave the peace of the countryside, but was very ill-prepared for such a move. Like so many other country boys, he could see no other way before him if he wanted to earn more. There was social injustice in rural and industrial areas, but the miner was at least better paid than the farm worker. Many farmhands were inadequately fed, and one old man related to me the way he used to watch the hens carefully when he worked on a Pembrokeshire farm as a boy—so that he could see where they laid their eggs. He would then take an egg or two, pierce a hole in the shell and suck the contents as quickly as he could so as not to be caught.

So it was that my father made up his mind to join his brothers in the Rhondda, where there was a dire shortage of men to dig out the much sought-after coal. The coal boom was at its height. He could see the way the Irish labourers who worked as navvies in Fishguard were squandering their money in a reckless fashion, whilst he was paid a mere pittance. There was nothing for it but to start a new life in the Rhondda.

He must have had mixed feelings about leaving his kind uncle and aunt, but at the same time it must have been a great comfort to know that some relatives and friends were already in Tylorstown. The journey he was undertaking was a long one by the standards of that period. It was his first-ever train journey. His personal belongings must have been very sparse and he would have to start work immediately to ensure having the basic needs of life. Securing food, clothing and shelter was all that he could hope to achieve and he would certainly have been contented with that much.

By the time he arrived, William, his brother, had found him lodgings, and the following morning he and an old friend walked to Ferndale. He entered the Ferndale Hotel with a put-on swagger and ordered two pints of beer—which was one penny a pint! He soon emptied his glass and unthinkingly placed it upside down on the counter. His friend consequently hurried him out of the Ferndale Hotel which was thronged with young miners. By placing his glass on the table as he had, he had unwittingly issued a challenge to fight the best man in the room! They hastily walked back to Tylorstown where he noticed that men who were building the *Duke of York Hotel* were busily engaged in putting the ground floor window-sills in position.

The following day, he accompanied his brother William to the pit-head to watch him enter the cage before it descended, taking him to pit bottom for the afternoon shift. Whilst he was speaking to William, the cage suddenly went on its way, and my poor inexperienced father instinctively bent forward to look after it as it went down the shaft. Bang! Down came the heavy iron safety-device. He was startled and badly shaken by the resounding metallic thud which could have ended his life. The huge shutter missed him by inches. What an introduction to coal mining—but it taught him that he had to keep himself alert to danger in his new environment!

He must have longed for the tranquillity of the countryside as he stood in the midst of coal-dust and noise and complex pit-head machinery moving trams of loaded or empty trams, and quick-moving men who looked like black demons. He had never known the love of caring parents and had no home in Pembrokeshire. He had learnt that conditions, hard and strange as they were, had to be accepted. As he stood in the midst of this inferno of steam and black dust, he might have regretted having chosen coal-mining.

He was not happy with machines, although, admittedly, he worked in a ship's engine-room later in life. The companionship of horses was preferable, he felt. I remember him relating a story about himself working alone in a field, in the stillness of the countryside, when he heard a strange noise gradually drawing nearer. Looking in its direction, he saw the head and shoulders of the local doctor moving across the top of the far hedge. My father ran to a distant gate, and arrived in time to see the doctor pass by in his newly acquired car. The 'horseless carriage' had arrived.

But he now found himself in the immense work-force of the famous South Wales coalfield. William taught him how to extract coal and how to take the essential safety precautions at the coal-face. The money was good and he loved the full life of a tough miner. He made his family ashamed to own him by behaving badly in drink on the paddle-steamer trip to Weston, but this was not in keeping with his character. He was only finding his feet, and within a few years of this episode he was a chapel deacon. Some summer nights, after a Saturday of enjoying himself in the Rhondda Fawr, he would sleep on the benches on Penrhys and return to his lodgings on Sunday morning. What he had been taught in the village school and the good influence of regular chapel-going were very important in deciding what kind of adult he

End of the afternoon shift.

wanted to be. In a short time he had made up his mind that he wanted to be a sober, responsible person.

During his first few years in the Rhondda he was a 'lodger'. Practically every home in the Rhondda valleys augmented the weekly income by keeping a lodger. These lodgers formed a significant part of Rhondda society and the ones I remember were quiet, hard-working types who became 'part of the family' as the years went by. Some never married and were contentedly settled in their bachelor ways. They remained in the same household until they died, but even so I felt sorry for them.

My earliest memory of my father is of being held by him to see a heavy snowfall that he had begun to clear from the front of the house. My mother was standing behind him. He was tall and strong, fresh-complexioned and blue-eyed. I do not remember him as a coal-miner, but I have fleeting glimpses of my mother preparing the bath tub in mid-afternoon, ready for his return from the morning shift. She was a very methodical person and this would be accomplished with little fuss.

His first sea voyage took him away from home for two years, but he had stocked enough coal and cut enough wood to last that time. The wooden sticks had been cut from blocks he had brought home from the colliery, and they had all been cut to size so that they fitted easily into the grate. Coal was stacked neatly in two places in addition to the coal-house—one pile opposite the kitchen window. The sweet smell of coal-gas remained for some time after he had left for his new life, and I could not understand why. His miner's clothes and tools lay in neat piles, unused, while the jack for water and the food-box for sandwiches were both in the *cwtsh* under the stairs. The very large garden on the mountain slope between us and the next terrace remained unkempt during his absence. Sadly, I realise now that my father had left for the sea before I was old enough to remember him, and I knew him only from the fleeting visits between trips. In his early forties, he had faced the difficult choice of being unemployed at home, or taking the opportunity of having regular employment and being far away for most of the time. He was fortunate to have the offer.

He had been injured in a very dangerous roof-fall when he was in No. 9 Colliery. A heavy rock fell near him and the edge of it landed on his boot. He was unable to get his foot clear, and his brother Frank and others were unable to lift the rock. There was no time to lose because the sure signs were that a severe roof fall was impending. Ominous drippings of fire-dust kept falling from the roof, which was clear

Pont-y-gwaith from Llanwonno Road.

indication that it was too dangerous to stay there. Frank, resourceful in times of emergency, grabbed a sledge-hammer and, telling my father to grit his teeth in expectation of severe pain, swung the hammer with heavy well-placed swings onto the rock. Many swings were made and each heavy thud sent spasms of pain through my father's foot and leg. At last, and to everybody's relief, the stone eventually cracked and my father was freed. Minutes after he had been carried out to safety, the main fall took place. Frank would have died with my father. The other helpers were standing away in safety whilst the stone was being cracked but they also were in danger when they rushed into the 'stall' to carry my injured father to the 'road' where the 'journeys' were running to the pit-bottom.

The accident rate was much higher than it is these days. Bravery and self-sacrifice in an attempt to save others was part of the mining tradition. Somewhere in the coalfield, there was possibly a heroic deed every day, which went unnoticed, except by those directly involved. On this particular occasion, my father's boot was removed in the First Aid room and he was carried from there through the streets to Church Street, my mother having been forewarned of his being brought home injured. Kind neighbours rushed to the house and assisted in bringing a bed from upstairs to the pleasant bay-windowed front room. Water was prepared, and arrangements made to soften the blow for the children when they returned from school—they would have their tea with their neighbour's children. There was no Welfare State benefit system in those days and my parents would henceforth have very little money to carry them through the difficult times ahead.

Dr. Morris had been called to the house. He immediately amputated a toe and in the course of the next few weeks had to amputate two others. For almost ten months my father was out of work, but he was permanently disabled, although he was at all times reluctant to admit it. He walked only with difficulty. My mother always encouraged him to stand erect and to walk as smartly as possible. Indeed years went by before he deigned to tell me of his disability—I was shocked to see his foot with only the big and little toe left. It was a relief for my father to be passed fit enough to work in the colliery—he would not ask for compensation because, if it were granted, he would certainly lose his job. Friends of his who had been injured too severely to be employed again, were finding life difficult on the meagre compensation they had been given. He knew only too well that he could lose his job, as well as any compensation, if he made a fuss, because the company might say that the fall of rock was caused by his own negligence. Some years before, the manager had told him to make the roof of his 'stall' safer, but he had not done so. When the manager came round again he noticed that new supports had not been put to make the roof safe and he was naturally annoyed with my father. Fortunately, the manager's wife and my mother had been brought up in New Quay, Dyfed, and this saved my father from being disciplined on the second telling. Naturally, there would be no third chance and the roof was made safe.

When my father suffered the accident, unemployment in the coal industry was increasing. The Royal Navy had forsaken coal for oil and the Merchant Navy was following the same path. Exports were falling alarmingly and the future looked bleak. The best that my father could do, under the circumstances, was to continue to say little about his accident and resume work quietly so as not to attract undue attention to himself. This would not be difficult for my father who was of a quiet and placid disposition.

However, my mother's brothers were sea captains, and one of them, Captain D. R. Williams, made arrangements for my father to become a stoker on a Royal Mail passenger-ship. Apparently, miners did not make good stokers, but I never heard my father complain later in life about his time in the stokeholds. Although miners were necessarily strong and tough, they were unable to keep up with the fast pace of stokers. The following trip, he was transferred to an oil-burning Royal Mail vessel and on one occasion, whilst serving on this ship, he came home with a bandaged arm and chest. He had been caught in a blast of hot steam from a faulty valve. Yet, he was healthy and made a rapid recovery so that he was fit to join the ship when she sailed.

On his first leave, my father took me to the pay-office of No. 9 Colliery. It was Friday, the miners' pay-day. Many were in their working clothes and a significant difference from the present-day miner was that they wore cloth caps (known as 'Dai caps' in the mining valleys of South Wales) and not the now familiar helmet. This was the last occasion that he went to a pit-head. Despite having to leave home and his beloved chapel, he much preferred being a seafarer. Soon he was fortunate to have work on the S.S. *Ruperra* sister ship to the *Ravenshoe* and the *Ramillies*. The latter ships were captained by his brother-in-law and my brother Ivor became third mate of the first ship and second mate of the second vessel.

Unloading at New Quay pier.

Chapter 2

My mother was born in 1882 in the small, busy port of New Quay, Cardiganshire (now part of the much larger administrative authority of Dyfed). Traditionally there were fishermen living in these parts from early times, in small cottages whose gardens probably stretched down towards the sands of Traeth Gwyn. The sturdy herring-boats, which had been developed from smaller craft over the long unchanging centuries, were built locally from the thickly forested land. Cultivating some coastal land and fishing for mackerel and herring in their season meant that these people were self-sufficient, but the rich land and sea harvests had to be carefully preserved and salted in readiness for the winter, if they were to survive.

This stretch of coastline, like the rest of Wales, was difficult to administer from London. The few roads that entered Wales were little better than cart tracks in many areas and, the further west one travelled, communications became more difficult. Thick layers of mud halted and trapped horses and men and embedded wheels so deeply that teams of horses had to be fetched from nearby farms to haul them out. Flooding, deep snowdrifts and lurking highwaymen were further dangers which made a journey to London a dangerous and uncomfortable venture.

The hinterland was only sparsely populated and there were fewer villages than one would find in England. Apart from a few market towns, the habitations consisted largely of scattered farms and cottages. It was sheltered anchorage for fishing boats and room for a few cottages that attracted the early settlers to New Quay—there was a reef which gave some protection from rough seas, and further shelter was provided by Pencraig Head. When New Quay was being established, the streets had to be built in terraces which cut into the steep headland, and consequently I found the place to be as steep as the Rhondda villages.

My interest in the village is entirely due to the fact that my mother's family had lived there for 250 years, and I was certainly more appreciative of the natural beauty of New Quay and of family tradition, because I did not live there. During my stay there, the day would be spent in the company of contemporaries, cousins and friends, but in the evenings I listened to the conversations of my elders, when they met in each other's houses. Some years I would stay in New Quay until the middle of September, and then I would sit quietly by my grandfather's side on the high-backed wooden bench, the *sgiw*, which was near the culm fire, hoping that I would not be noticed and sent to bed. As I grew older, I became more impressionable and wanted to believe, rightly or wrongly, that we were descended on my grandmother's side from the early fisher-folk, who lived in the isolated cottages that were dotted along the coast. I believed that my ancestors had lived for centuries where New Quay now stands, even before it was established as a small but busy sea port, and concluded that this hypothesis was probably true, because a search of parish records was to show that the family lived in the area as long ago as 1720, and people did not usually leave their locality in those days.

I heard my elders say that, once New Quay was established, the inhabitants were identified by a family name or nickname which, after a few decades, would embrace scores of people and show how they were related. The following are some old New Quay families I heard of when listening to fireside conversations:

y Phillipiaid — The Phillips family
y Morganiaid — The Morgan family
y Timothiaid — The Timothy family
y Gofion — The blacksmiths
y Cryddion — The shoemakers.

There were many others which I did not hear sufficiently often to remember.

Kinship was important in Welsh family life. I was told that I was a member of the Phillips family. They were not prominent, but I was very pleased to be somewhere on this family tree and probably experienced the same pride as a Scotsman who discovers that he belongs to a clan. I discovered that an old aunt called Kate Davies was well-acquainted with the intricacies of family relationships and, being the youngest of her generation, she was an invaluable link with my past.

The family was given a nickname which I did not particularly like when I first heard it. It was 'Cadnoid', the Welsh for 'foxes'. I subsequently discovered that animal names were given to groups of people so that a person could be jokingly called, for instance, a 'Pembrokeshire pig' or an 'Aberdare snake'. I happened to discuss the term 'Cadnoid' with a cousin when we were fishing off New Quay; contrary to my opinion, he did not think the custom was meant to be offensive: indeed, he seemed pleased with the choice of animal for our family. I

"Cadno"

could only secretly feel grateful that we had not been given a worse name!

Owing to the isolation of the community and the increase in population towards the end of the nineteenth century, third cousins often married each other. In the first half of the twentieth century, for example, two of my first cousins married third cousins of theirs. One reason for such practice seems to have been that people who did not live near railways found it very difficult to travel, and consequently when they mixed with the opposite sex, their choice of a partner, if marriage was contemplated, was limited. That marriage of near relatives did take place can be detected in blood characteristics. Such was the case with a second cousin of mine who took part in a clinical research project which discovered this fact as an incidental finding.

It was easier to travel by sea on a small schooner than to travel by road—despite the discomfort of being tossed and turned in a sailing-boat.

Smuggling was as much a serious problem along the Welsh coast as it was in Devon and Cornwall. Welsh and Irish pirates were a great menace and for centuries they had been feared by honest traders plying the Bristol Channel and Irish Sea. Wrecking was a cruel trick played on mariners who were lured by false lights fixed on dangerous coasts, and sometimes by two lights placed at opposite ends of a donkey which would then be walked on cliff paths. The unsuspecting sailors would assume that the moving and swaying lights were from a vessel in safe waters. They would navigate their ship towards the lights and to their doom. Men, women and children would line the shore waiting for the inevitable disaster and, when it happened, grab everything of value, leaving the poor victims to their fate. It was safer for the wreckers that there should be no survivors to relate of the incidents leading up to the shipwreck.

Most coastal people felt that smuggling, wrecking and a little piracy went hand-in-hand with lawful occupations such as fishing and trading. My Uncle David—Captain D. R. Williams, Hafan Dawel—once pointed towards Traeth Gwyn and told me that some of the family lived in cottages that have since been swamped by the sea and covered by sand. "They were possibly the wreckers," he said, "and the family controlled the beach before shipbuilding was started in earnest." I would have questioned him further but an old farm-worker came by and I was introduced to him. The conversation turned from the sea to life on a farm when the old man, now ninety years old, was a youth.

When we moved on, my uncle pointed his walking-stick along the coast from Cei Bach to Pencraig and away towards Llangrannog and said, "That's where Joseph Jones* patrolled, assisted by seventeen armed men, to stop the smuggling of salt." I was still a schoolboy, but old enough to appreciate the significance of what he had said. I knew the narrow cliff-top path to Llangrannog like the back of my hand, but only in fine clear weather. Now I imagined the Excise Officer struggling in stormy weather to complete his difficult patrol. If it was summer time, he would pass fields of yellow corn behind stone walls on one side and, on the other, soft green grass leading to the edge of steep cliffs. Sometimes the path would lead right to the cliff edge and, the last time I walked there alone, I feared the sheer drop and turned back. The sea was far below and, on one occasion, a friend who lived in London House hailed me from his small boat. He had stopped the outboard engine and was fishing. He cupped his hands and called my name, then asked if I was all right. We were both alone, he on the calm sea and I on the cliff top, between New Quay and Llangrannog.

The era of shipbuilding brought craftsmen to New Quay where schooners were designed and built. We were sailors, and when the craftsmen had finished their building work, we sailed them, and, as was the custom, joined with others to buy the vessels. Small companies

* Joseph Jones, my great-great-great-great-grandfather, 1759-1839, was an Excise Officer in New Quay.

Shipbuilding at Cei-bach.

were formed and shares in a schooner was good business. My family was known as Jenkin Phillips and they traded under that name. There were dozens of similar companies in New Quay, and to meet the demand hundreds of sailing-ships were built in New Quay, Traeth Gwyn and Cei Bach.

Wire ropes and rusting chains, an encrusted crane and solid iron hoops strongly embedded in walls and cliffs, were a few reminders of past industry. Old ships' names were still mentioned in conversation. One of them was the *Ann Warren* which was captained by John James. She was built in 1857 on Traeth Gwyn, and captured my interest in the first instance because she traded under a company called Jenkin Phillips. She was sold in 1904 to a Gloucester firm where she was used on the River Severn to carry goods from Bristol to Gloucester. She was last seen moored to a wharf in Gloucester, stripped of her rigging and reduced to a hulk.

Herring-fishing was still the occupation of some New Quay men when they tired of long, deep-sea voyages, and this did not cease until the end of the Second World War. I was fortunate, when I was young, that a relative of mine partly owned the *Hope*, the only black-hulled fishing boat in New Quay (black being the traditional colour of Cardiganshire herring-boats). Most of the other boats were painted white with black lettering and numerals, showing their registration. The crew of the *Hope* consisted of three, one of whom had been a ship's engineer and who managed to keep the engine running smoothly. The boat had a tall mast and splendid sails—so we were not totally relying on the skills of the Scottish engineer, who nevertheless kept wiping the engine over. There was a smell of petrol and oil and fish and tobacco which, when combined with the motion of the boat and the harsh noise of the engine, challenged the constitution of the best of landlubbers. I was too young to be taken out in rough weather and consequently never experienced seasickness. My relative, whom I knew as Uncle John 'Oriel', had been a boatswain with my mother's brother, Captain D. R. Williams, on the various ships he had commanded. He had lost sight in one eye when the ship was attacked in the First World War and a splinter from the wooden deck had pierced it. Ever since, he had worn a black clasp over the damaged eye and this, combined with his good looks and general toughness, gave him an almost theatrical appearance when he steered the *Hope* out into Cardigan Bay.

I have a vivid recollection of being taken on a fishing trip in the early hours of the morning. This had been planned by my grandfather and John 'Oriel', much against the wishes of my grandmother and mother, because I was only eight years old. A handful of gravel was thrown across my bedroom window—I can still remember the light, swishing sound that woke me as handfuls of gravel brushed lightly across the small window panes. My grandfather, who slept in the room below, was awakened in the same manner, and he knocked at the oak beams above his bed with his walking stick to make sure that I was awake. The old man, now approaching eighty years of age, would have enjoyed this fishing trip and would, I'm sure, have survived it if he had been carried to the boat. He had taken great interest in seeing that I was well-prepared for the fishing adventure. It was still dark and somewhat chilly, so he made sure that I had a good muffler and woollen cap, whilst my mother gave me a hot cup of tea. Out at sea, my uncle offered me hot tea, without sugar and milk, from a flask and said it was beer. My mother, being of a more religious disposition, was annoyed when I told her that I enjoyed drinking beer and scolded my uncle when she next met him.

Some years later, he joined with other New Quay men and became their boatswain on a voyage which proved to be his last one. When the trip was practically over and the ship was unloading in London, he went shopping in the West End. As he was looking in a shop window, a van, which had gone out of control, mounted the pavement and killed him; his friend, who was beside him, was unscathed. The *Hope* was eventually sold and taken away from New Quay, and as the other fishermen died, the fishing boats became fewer, and the direct link with the original occupation of the people was soon to disappear. First, it had been herring-fishing, which lasted for centuries until the nineteenth century, when there was shipbuilding and trading, and that also was to be eventually replaced by holidaymakers. My family were involved in the three phases and were among the last of the old-style fishermen.

Voyaging to the Bay of Biscay must have been dreaded by New Quay families because many ships were lost in these stormy seas. One of my grandmother's uncles was drowned as his schooner passed that way. I saw a painting of him in New Quay, yellowed by varnish and age, which showed him to be a dark-haired man, deeply tanned and keen-eyed. In the bottom right-hand corner, a diminutive schooner had been painted depicting the vessel which was lost with all hands. I was also shown an article in a monthly magazine for children, *Trysorfa'r Plant*, giving an account of the death and subsequent events of a New Quay sea-captain who was one of the family. He had taken his wife on a long voyage which took them to India where he died of some mysterious illness.

My great-grandfather was Captain David Jones from Llan-non. I was told that when the *Ann Warren* was launched in 1857, and owned by his father-in-law, Jenkin Phillips, he was the captain. His life was to conclude tragically in 1869 when he drowned in Plymouth harbour. Mystery surrounds his death: his body was never found, but his

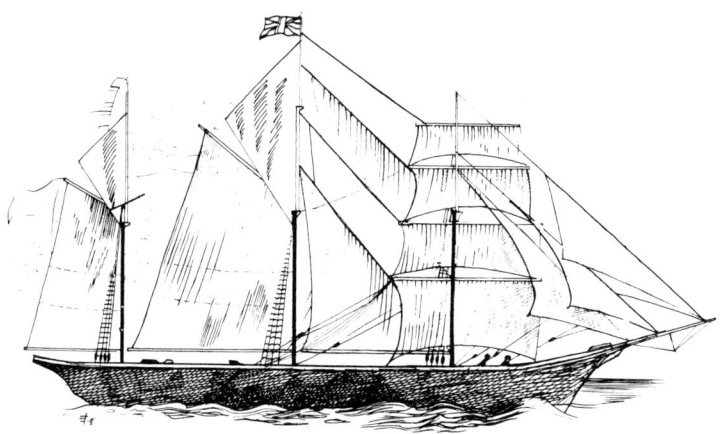

New Quay schooner.

Fishing-boats.

master-mariner's top-hat was seen floating in the water. Many questions were asked at the inquiry. But he was attested to be a sober, good-living man, so it is improbable that he slipped and fell into the water. No cries or scuffles were heard and he was thus not missed until morning when his cabin was found to be empty. His name is engraved on the gravestone in New Quay churchyard, together with that of his wife and daughter and son-in-law.

Families were identified by the ships they owned or in which they sailed. Some captains named their houses, others their children, after their ships. Thus we have Warren after the *Ann Warren* and Ivor after the schooner *Ifor*. My mother, Elizabeth Jane, was named after a schooner owned by Jenkin Phillips, and my sister, Morwen, after an open herring-boat which my grandfather owned in addition to a partly closed-deck fishing-boat. *Ifor* was a Jenkin Phillips' schooner.

Increasing activity in the small shipyards, and closer links with Northern European and Mediterranean ports, opened up new avenues for expansion. The horizons widened still further and voyages were undertaken in locally-built ships, to America, Australia, India and even to China. It was part of the optimism, self-assurance and feeling of superiority that was typical of Queen Victoria's reign. Many small ports were improved to meet the new demands that were being placed on them, and the New Quay Harbour Act was passed on 12th June

1835 in the reign of William IV. Two years later the Victorian era began and the new monarch was on the throne until 1901. The village expanded until, by 1870, it was so well established that it was little changed until the time when I first remember it in 1925. As many as 200 ships were built in New Quay and the adjacent beaches in the first ten years after the pier was completed. At the height of this activity and enthusiasm, the peace of rural Rhondda was beginning to be disturbed by Walter Coffin and others. As New Quay pier was being built, its commercial doom was being sealed in the Rhondda where the first shafts were being sunk. The busy little ports were going to be short-lived when the great Bristol Channel ports were built to handle the export of Rhondda coal. The South Wales coalfield soon had an efficient network of railways to bring coal to the great docks, so that New Quay, by the end of the century, was reduced to a holiday resort.

The pier cost £7,000, which was far less than the sum asked for in the first place—in the early plans; that pier, if built, would have been very much bigger than the present one. The money for the construction of the pier was raised by forming a company, well-known people being happy to be main shareholders in the venture. The project was regarded as a sound investment which would be a permanent business-necessity for New Quay, but it turned out to be otherwise, because before the end of the century the pier was not being used as often as it used to be. I remember it being said that the shareholders were frustrated—their money was tied up in a pier which brought them no profit to be paid out in dividends, and which could not be sold. Holiday-makers promenaded and sunbathed on it and New Quay benefitted generally because the pier gave the resort its distinctive appearance and appeal. Material for its construction was quarried at the far end of New Quay, at Pencraig. The huge stones were floated to the pier or carried on a specially-constructed railway which ran along the cliff top from the quarry. (Later, Rock Street was constructed on the site which had been cleared for the line.) Farm-horses and their drivers were employed in moving the stones.

The quarry was still being used when I was a boy, and loud explosions resounding throughout the sleepy village would send startled seagulls screaming out to sea and halt the interesting conversations of gossiping women enjoying the summer sunshine. If one was near enough, the splashes of hundreds of small stones hurled high into the sky by the blast could be heard as they fell into the calm sea. Men and boys were constantly warned not to steer their boats near Pencraig quarry, and a red flag warned pedestrians of the same danger.

" . . . startled seagulls screaming out to sea."

Through the centuries ships had anchored in the sheltered waters of what was a natural harbour, but from Tudor times there was a steady increase in Welsh prosperity and a pattern of regular trading was established in New Quay. A small quay known as 'Penpolion' was built in the eighteenth century, constructed of large rocks and flat stones, marked by long poles, which showed its position whatever the state of the tide. It was a splendid place to find crabs. The rocks and the bottom end of the pier slipway were also thick with seaweed and jellyfish, but during a recent visit I noticed their almost complete absence due to sea pollution.

1. Captain David Jones (my great grandfather) with his family

2. *3rd from right* Robert Williams (my grandfather). *6th from right* Captain D. R. Williams (my uncle)

3. Captain D. R. Williams
(*cf.* 2)

4. Captain W. Ivor Davies
(my brother)

5. SS *Roath*—D. R. Williams' first command

6. SS *Ravenshoe*, captained by D. R. Williams, which my brother, Captain Ivor Davies, joined as a boy of fourteen

7. Captain Ivor Williams (*centre*).
He was presented by President Wilson
with a pair of binoculars bearing the
following citation "From the President
of the United States to E. I. Williams,
Chief Officer of the British Steamship
Mombassa, in recognition of his heroic
services at sea, on January 17th 1915, to
the Master and Crew of the American
schooner Alice Lord."

8. M.V. *British Comet*, one of the B.P. oil tankers commanded by Capt. William Ivor Davies

9. "It never crossed my mind that I would see Tylorstown without its collieries."

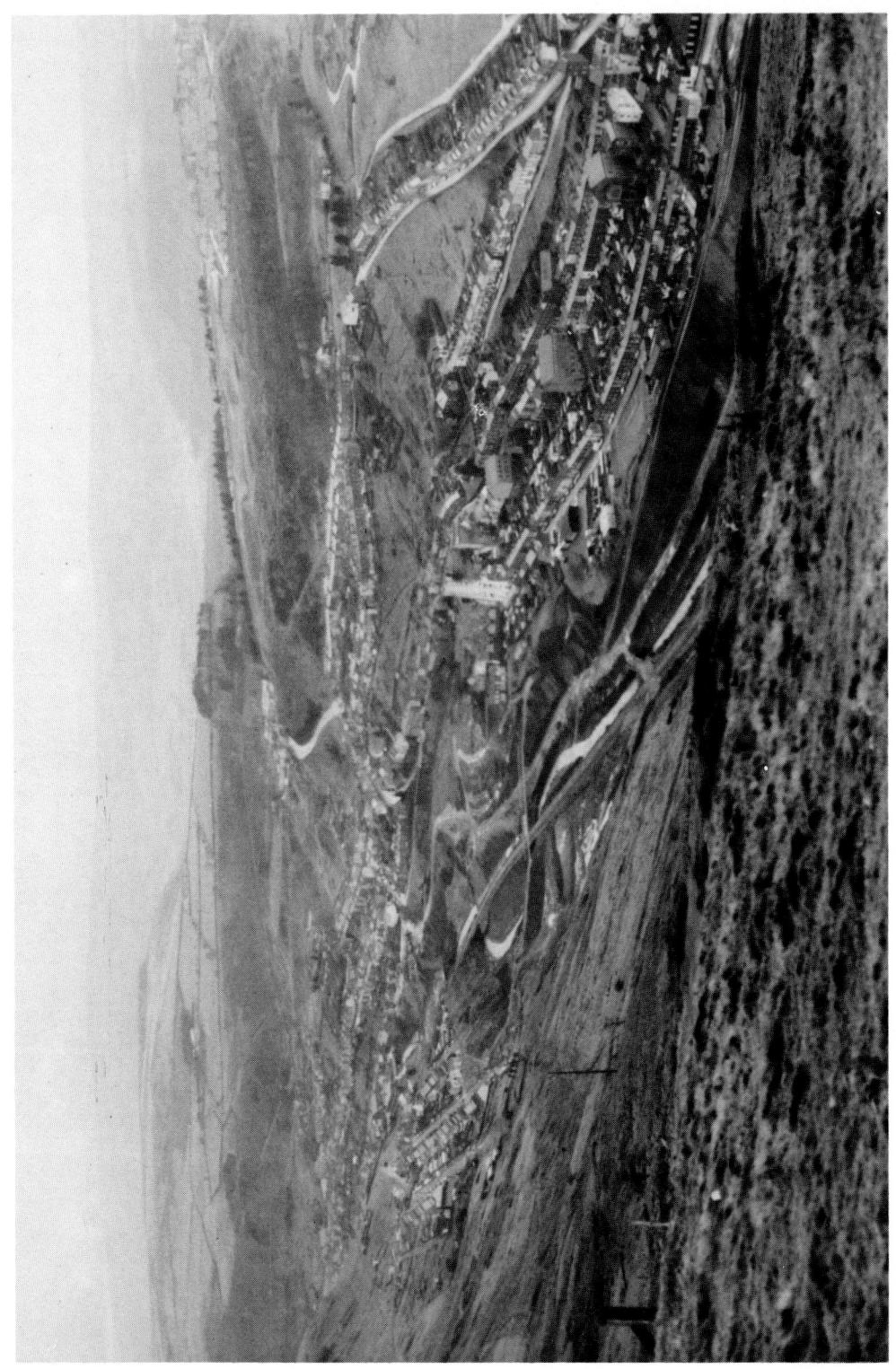

My friends learned about the sea and how to handle boats at a young age. By ten years of age they could sail small boats, row and scull with ease, swim and dive expertly, tie good knots, catch fish and generally maintain their rowing-boats. Tylorstown boys left school at thirteen-and-a-half and started work in the local collieries, whereas New Quay boys of the same age became 'cabin boys' on tramp steamers. My two brothers, although reared in Tylorstown, went to sea and served under their uncles who were captains of ocean-going vessels. My eldest brother celebrated his fourteenth birthday 2,000 miles up the River Amazon! Both boys became officers in the Merchant Service.

When my grandmother moved to the lonely cottage on a road which led from New Quay to the heart of the country, it must have been a hard wrench for her as well as her mother. My grandmother, recalling those days, said that one day a bearded, ragged and dirty tramp knocked at the cottage door, begging for food and money. She succeeded in getting rid of him by saying that her father was at the back of the house, and called her deceased father's name so urgently that she expected him to appear. Having enjoyed the privileges of being a captain's daughter, she now had to learn to take the hard knocks of life. She was never to become financially comfortable again, a situation which must have been all the more difficult for her to bear as she saw her relatives free of money-worries. From 1842 to the end of the century, life was unkind to the family because of the loss, in middle

New Quay pier.

33

age, of the bread winners. Both were master-mariners. In fact, three generations suffered setbacks, but they refused to capitulate to their difficulties.

I was taken to see people who lived in a cottage which was on the same country lane as the one my grandmother moved to when her father died. This family had been very kind and considerate. Their small, thatched cottage, with its tiny windows set in white-washed stone walls, had an adjoining field or two in which they kept a cow, chickens, and a few ducks; they supplied us with milk and eggs. The family was now reduced to the pretty woman, called Mary Jones, and her bed-ridden father whom she was looking after.

On my first visit, which was to fetch the evening milk, her father was lying peacefully in a large four-poster bed which took up half the room. It was known in the locality that the doctor had confirmed that the old man had only a few days to live, so my sister and cousin Phyllis had asked if I could accompany them to the house. My cousin, who was high-spirited, teased me about my uses as a bodyguard. My sister was nervous and afraid of the dark.

The light was failing when we reached the cottage, and the fire glowed brightly in the old-fashioned grate; there was an autumnal chill in the evening air. The room looked comfortable in the lamplight and everything was prepared for the long, lonely vigil. The room had been partitioned with a wooden screen which had a neat latched door set in one of the panels. This was the windowless bedroom where Mary Jones had her privacy.

We collected the lidded enamel jug of still-warm milk which would be used at breakfast time, and stepped out into the gathering dusk. It was almost dark when we had said goodnight and we could see the moon rising out of Cardigan Bay through the leafy gaps in the trees and hedges. My sister had been upset when she saw the old man propped on his many pillows, but I had thought that he looked peaceful. His snow-white hair, red face and long white beard, which had been draped neatly outside the bed clothes, reminded me of Father Christmas. Phyllis, who had gone closer to the bed than my sister so that she could have a better look, made her more nervous by pointing at queer witch-like shapes in the hedges. There was a cool sea-breeze which moved the shapes and rustled the dying leaves. Fine swarms of late midges made our way difficult because a herd of cows had recently passed by and messed the country lane. A swooping bat, and teasing Phyllis talking about the spirits of the dead, made us hasten. The girls came closer and real fright began to grip us. It was a relief to arrive at the kissing-gate which led to Creiglan, where Phyllis lived and where we were staying. Night had fallen, but the old man lived through it. He died before the year was out, and when I was taken to the cottage the next summer, the four-poster bed had been removed and Mary was alone. She had invited us to tea so that she would have the opportunity to thank my mother for reading the Bible and praying with her father the previous summer. Tea had been prepared and placed on a three-legged round table which had a chequered red and white tablecloth; everything we ate was delicious. The bread and cakes had been freshly baked and Mary had made her own butter and jam. She wanted to discuss another problem with my mother and I was asked to feed the hens. The news reached us in Tylorstown some months later that she had died of cancer. The cottage remained empty. Nobody wanted it and when, some years later, curiosity led me to it, I found a heap of stones and tall grass marking the perimeter.

More years went by and I discovered that the country lane had been widened and properly surfaced. Street lamps had been erected and houses built along the road, and the cottage had been replaced by a smart bungalow. As if to make sure that I would accept that the old lifestyle had gone for ever, a big dusty car filled with happy holiday-makers roared past me and headed for the still unspoilt country.

I loved listening to the men home from the sea.

I loved listening to the men home from the sea who always had 'a yarn to spin' about their voyages. Wartime adventures were not the only stories which held my interest. My cousin's husband told me that David Livingstone had presented a silver-topped walking-stick to his grandfather, to show his appreciation of the kindness shown him over the years when conveying him to Africa in the *Hetty Ellen* which sailed regularly to Africa and carried stores for the famous missionary. The walking stick is still with his relations.

I heard and read in the press about a young man who had been killed by Chinese pirates in the North China Sea. He was a junior officer on the vessel which had been chartered to carry gold bullion for the Chinese government. Three large junks approached the ship and turned out to be manned by hostile Chinese. Their confederates were already on the vessel whose decks were crowded with Chinese passengers and their goods. As the bridge was being attacked, the junks came alongside and the pirates boarded the ship. In the firing, the young officer, who was from New Quay and was a relative, was killed and his body was thrown into the sea. The captain and officers were locked in their rooms and the ship drifted helplessly until it was located by a British warship which was searching for it. Another young relative was killed by a shark in a South American port when he was swimming near his anchored ship, and my cousin Roy drifted for hours in the Bristol Channel after his ship had been torpedoed between Barry and Llantwit Major, before being spotted and rescued. He clung to floating wreckage with one of his apprentices who tragically had to give up the ordeal and, despite Roy's words of encouragement, finally slipped under the waves.

Another cousin, named Danny, first-mate of the *Salvus*, went ashore at Freetown by ship's launch, to see the shipping agents before leaving for Cape Town. He died of blackwater fever before the ship had docked in Cape Town. At the early age of twenty-four, he had passed his captain's certificate and was set for a good career. My brother Ivor had the rare experience of having his ship torpedoed on two occasions. The first time was in Trinidad harbour when many ships were struck and the second occasion some weeks later when the ship was proceeding to New York for more extensive repairs. This time the ship foundered and he was in the lifeboat for several days. The ship had taken a long time to sink and he had returned to his cabin to fetch his sextant. The deck was almost level with the sea and he was able to step from the lifeboat onto the sinking vessel. Later the captain rebuked him for taking the lifeboat back to the stricken vessel which could have foundered at any time. Many of the family were on the Russian convoys and miraculously all but one survived. My father's old ship was torpedoed at two minutes to midnight and sank within a few minutes with only a handful of survivors.

Loaded tankers were placed on the outside lane of convoys so that as they exploded, if struck by torpedo, they were less liable to place other ships in danger. A relative told me of the horror of having to leave a sister ship—one of the fleet of British Tankers that was engulfed in flames. The sea was ablaze around the stricken ship and he could hear the screams of tortured dying men who on other trips had been his shipmates. Their last struggles were witnessed from the decks of the passing ship. It was a bitter, soul-searing experience to watch helplessly and obey the rules of wartime convoys which forbade ships to stop and help.

During these dark forbidding days of war, Dylan Thomas came to New Quay and stayed for many months in a bungalow in a narrow country lane that led to Traeth Gwyn. At one time, this had been the road to Cei Bach but the sea had encroached so that it now ended on a soft clay bank which bordered the beach. It was in New Quay that the first inspiration and planning of *Under Milk Wood* took place. Fortunately the harshness of war did not stop his creative genius, and, as millions suffered and died, a literary work of eternal beauty was being created.

Chapter 3

The towering mountain slag heap.

I was born and brought up in Tylorstown in a community far removed from the maritime tranquillity of New Quay, Cardiganshire. I lived in a valley community which, like every other in the civilised world, was facing great changes owing to new inventions which were being placed at the disposal of ordinary people. The bewildering rapidity of these scientific advances was already dramatically altering the character of Rhondda communities, which had come into being only sixty to seventy years previously. There had been little time to consolidate before new social challenges had to be met. The decline of the coal industry in the Rhondda began twenty years after my father arrived from the country, and if one considered long-term prospects, his coming to the Rhondda had proved to be pointless by the time he was forty years of age.

Tylorstown consists of long lines of terraced houses, large compared with the earliest miners' cottages built in the Rhondda. From the mountain the cleverness of the builders can be appreciated, with the long, grey-stone, slate-roofed streets overlooking the four collieries which had brought us all to the locality. Our own comfortable home was built on one side of the valley, so that from our front rooms we looked at the other green, fern-clad side, which sloped steeply from the river bank, but was, unfortunately, crowned by an enormous pile of slag which had been dumped in the mountain-top fields skirted by the parish road to Llanwonno. The scene was a mixture of heavy industry and vestiges of rural beauty.

This towering mountain-top slag heap dominated Tylorstown, and in my boyhood days it was made even higher by the addition of a huge pyramid of coal waste. Because of this addition, some streets lost an hour or two of morning sunshine. The mine owners, however, showed little concern for the complaints made by a few of the residents.

My parents, who were honest, good-living people, had sincere religious convictions and were devoted to their chapel in Pont-y-gwaith, a Welsh Baptist chapel called Hermon, situated close to the river and railway which ran parallel to each other. When I was a few weeks old, I was wrapped in a shawl and taken, with my sister and two brothers, to Hermon, and from that time on until I left home, I never missed attending chapel on Sunday. This was the custom of the day, and I must confess that I found it irksome and the language of the service was well over my head. There was a good gathering in most services, and the natural language of my parents' generation was Welsh. That generation had left West Wales to populate the hitherto rural emptiness of the Rhondda Fach, and they were the first-time occupiers of the houses, the founders of the chapels, and the parents of large families which over-filled the schools. However, English was the natural language of the younger generation.

Rhondda homes were busy from morning to night, the focal point being the kitchen. I can remember huge loaves of delicious fresh bread which had been taken to one of the many bakehouses in the village. A very fierce woman baked our bread; her language was very rough-and-ready and the children, waiting to collect the big loaves, half-loved and half-feared her. She charged a penny or two for baking in tins clearly marked by the owner; we had H.D., the initials for Hugh Davies, on our tins. When she saw our tin of bread, she would shout, "B..... chapel people". She always wore a 'Dai cap' and was a typical Rhondda character. But her bark was worse than her bite, and we all knew that underneath her rough ways there was a heart of gold.

In the homes where the father and his sons were miners, the housewife worked very hard. Roaring kitchen fires were needed in the heat of summer as well as in winter time, to ensure a good supply of boiling water. Shift-work meant that as one of the family got out of bed to go to work, another was about to arrive for his bath, meal and sleep, and an

Houses in Tylorstown on the steep sided valley.

aunt of mine who had a very large family, because she had been twice married, went through this performance three times a day. Before World War I, when some miners were earning good money, there was an excellent weekly income in that household. My mother and I often called there on Saturday night when my aunt had finished baking for the weekend. She baked her own bread, and once I counted six lovely tarts cooling in the pantry. There were five miners in that home, and three daughters who helped until they were married and set up their own homes.

In my younger days, school registers were full and, if the classroom was large enough, two classes would share it. In such conditions there had to be good order and discipline, as well as good understanding between teachers. A chapel pew was not long enough for the average family. It is amazing, really, how large families were reared so successfully in such small houses. It was difficult to ventilate a cellar house which had to be overheated by big coal fires. Most Tylorstown houses had rooms which rarely had the benefit of sunshine because of their location in the narrow steep-sided valley. Despite these difficulties, however, the homes were clean and tidy and the inhabitants were cheerful. The turn-out for Sunday chapel was a spectacle—young women and girls attractively attired, men and boys tidily clothed, and the older generations dressed in careful fashion.

Rhondda sheep wandered freely through the streets, wild-eyed and dirty grey, searching for cabbage leaves and potato peelings or anything else that took their fancy. They usually walked in single file, but could act separately and push their noses into ash buckets, leaving a trail of tipped rubbish through the street. Wise gardeners protected their gardens with high walls and fences! Fierce-looking rams would sometimes escort the ewes through the street. Despite the collieries, the Rhondda had certainly not lost touch completely with country life. In Church Street there were plenty of hens and little yellow chicks, and each morning the dawn was greeted with the crows of many cockerels. One neighbour kept ducks, another had two goats and there was a fine pigeon-loft in one of the large allotments. On the green banks there were plenty of fluttering cabbage-butterflies, and big bees and big red-eyed spiders could be teased out of their webbed holes by touching their webs with a small stick.

It was a thrilling sight to see a team of colliery horses pulling a cart-load of coal from the main road up Brynbedw Road. The gradient was very steep and they would pound the dirt, sending it flying in all directions, and dig their hooves into the unsurfaced road. An energetic little man with a long whip, which he cracked now and again, ran by their side as they tackled the hill. As the momentum increased, he shouted high-pitched encouragement in a language which only the horses understood and they responded by pulling and straining, using all their immense strength until their bodies steamed and their eyes flashed and bulged with effort. Somewhere up the long hill, the challenge was over and they were halted. By now, their soft nostrils would be quivering as they rested after their all-out response to commands from the little man who had encouraged them the whole way. With a sliding rumble and a final crash, the coal would now be dumped on the pavement and, if it was summer-time and the air was dry, clouds of black dust would fall about the horses and settle on their sticky, sweating bodies. When the delivery note had been signed, the haulier would lead the team of horses back to the coal 'stank' where another load would be put on the cart.

Members of the family, both young and old, would tackle the black heap on the pavement and carry it in laden buckets and specially designed skips used by the miners in their work. It would be an united effort and the coal was carried over neatly newspaper-covered floors,

Tylorstown power station with the incline in the background.

through the passage, the middle and back-kitchen to the coal-house or shed in the back of the house. When the carrying was completed and the lumps of coal stacked neatly, it was time to start clearing up the mess caused by tramping feet and flying dust. Hot water, bars of soap, hard scouring, and careful drying and dusting soon returned the house to normality.

An unforgettable sight which I remember was when we saw the lamps of a few hundred miners leaving the lamp-room for the pit-head, while others were leaving the cage which had hauled them from the black depths after finishing their shift. My uncle, who had been in chapel earlier that evening and was on the night-shift, had walked with us from his home perched on the hillside, where we had been having an after-chapel supper. From the road we looked down on the pit-head, and I heard my mother catch her breath as pity and concern swept over her. We watched my uncle walk down to the pit-head gear from where we could hear the heavy bang of safety doors and the clang of signal-bells.

From where we stood, the smell of coal-gas wafted up to us and combined with that of well-oiled machinery and greasy truck wheels, as well as that from puffing steam billowing out of the engine room, and the sweat of men and horses. The delicate night-scented air from the dark heather and fern-clad mountain mingled with this to form a distinctive Rhondda colliery smell which I have not experienced elsewhere.

I never found out what exactly was being shouted from the incline, which went in a straight diagonal line on the side of the mountain from pit-head to the distant engine-house which looked so tiny from my house. Sometimes the shouting would come to me in the dark when I was playing hide-and-seek in the trees and bushes of the church grounds. I could tell by the urgency of the call that something had gone wrong. Usually it was that the trams had left the rails and help was needed to lift them back.

It never crossed my mind that I would see Tylorstown without a trace of its collieries. I had heard a local politician prophesy that people of my generation would live to see grass growing on the pit-heads, and the audience chuckled at the thought of any greenery growing on the four collieries. I tried hard to picture grass growing around the buildings and sidings but I would have been unable to imagine the rural appearance which has been made possible by massive, modern earth-moving machinery.

A community had been formed by bringing people to the Rhondda from different parts of Wales, Somerset and other places, but no sooner had it been fully brought together than the time came when it began to disintegrate. They had come to find work and better opportunities, and their grandchildren have been leaving the Rhondda for the same reasons ever since I can remember.

A colourful character, who never bothered to bring his horse and cart to the street where I lived because it was a waste of time, was the sand seller. He sold sand from the beaches which was used in turn by miners' wives to protect the floor after it had been scoured. Tylorstown streets, where he found no customers for his merchandise, were referred to by the sand man as 'carpet streets'. He spoke of them with disdain and, hearing him calling from afar, "Sand y môr" ('Sand from the sea'), I felt ashamed that my mother had linoleum or oilcloth on our kitchen floor.

My mother was very neat and tidy, and took pride in her home as did all our neighbours. Like the others, she saw nothing wrong in throwing unwanted vegetable leaves and potato and apple peelings onto the green bank. They would be there until the sheep came. 'Feeding the sheep' was a very handy way of getting rid of this unwanted food and someone said that Rhondda sheep produced tasty, good-flavoured mutton and lamb because of this habit. We also collected horse manure from the street and I remember my father having a load delivered from the colliery. This had been an annual order for many years, with the result that he had good growth in his allotment, although the gardens were on a steep slope and were difficult to cultivate.

Once, when he was old, he noticed that the grass in my back-garden wanted cutting. To help me overcome this task, which was difficult because I did not possess a lawn-mower for a small patch of grass, he guided three wandering sheep into the garden. When I arrived home from school, my first task was to get the sheep out of the garden—it took me half an hour with the help of my little collie dog. Unfortunately for me, however, a behaviour pattern had been set and sheep entered my garden for the rest of the time I lived in that house!

The fifty-three Rhondda collieries, which once employed 41,000 men, controlled everyday life with long wailing sounds from their hooters. Nowadays, radio and television give us correct times throughout the day, but in my young days the colliery-hooters were signals by which Rhondda clocks were synchronized. Each hooter sounded differently, and the nearest to my house was No. 9 colliery which had a low, husky tone. A knowledgeable older boy could tell from the pitch of the hooter from what colliery the sound came. From the mountain top, one could see puffs of white steam which preceded the sound of distant hooters.

Only once, fortunately, did I hear the frightening wail of the warning hooter which followed a strange muffled thud and stopped everybody in their tracks. On that particular occasion, there had been an explosion which killed many men at the coal-face. I was taking a lesson in a primary school when this happened, and a boy sitting in a front desk lost his father in the tragedy. He sat quietly through the remainder of the lesson after someone brought the news that several men were trapped at the coal-face.

It was when an elderly neighbour died that I first became aware of death. One of my friends, who was even younger than the rest of us, had lost his grandfather a few weeks previously, so that he was able to inform us that dying meant 'going to sleep for ever'.

I remember, on the day of the funeral, the crowd of bowler-hatted and black-suited men outside our house and, a few yards away, the two black horses adorned with mourning ribbons. They stood quietly and patiently in the shafts of the slender-wheeled glass hearse. A top-hatted man, who was vaguely familiar, officered the intricacies of bringing the coffin through the space made by the removal of a complete window-frame from the three-sided bay. I stared wide-eyed at what was, to me, a strange, inexplicable spectacle. After some Welsh prayers, the men struck up a funeral hymn. The voices were well trained, the harmonious blend thrilled me.

Although Tylorstown was a busy mining village, badly planned and hastily built, scarred with massive indiscriminate tipping of colliery waste, the open spaces were close at hand. A short climb brought one to a world of lonely, extensive, sheep-rearing country. I loved to escape from the noise, the coal-dust and the problems of growing up, by walking long distances across the hills. I never succeeded in finding a skylark's nest although I went to the right place in the grass where it had landed. When I became much older and attended grammar school, I enjoyed the company of a favourite girlfriend who had the same love of country walking. I had numerous girlfriends and my Art mistress teasingly remarked that I would have many wives! They were good-looking, intelligent girls and many have become life-long friends—and *one* my wife!

My father was not a follower of sport in the Rhondda Valley, but he had great interest in country sports such as horse riding and wrestling and often spoke of country-style, bare-fisted boxing. Physical strength impressed him and he once followed the career of a friend who was a champion weightlifter. This friend unfortunately died in a weightlifting exhibition in Pont-y-gwaith in which he had hoped to set a new record. My father was very upset when he spoke about this sad event because he had been present and was one of the crowd who had urged the poor man to lift the weights.

He kept clear of the tough characters who were mountain fighters. His brother John, who had settled in Abergwynfi, was a mountain fighter and nobody would dare disagree with him in the colliery. He spent a great deal of his life on his back after being paralysed by a roof fall underground. I never met him, but I remember my uncles from Tylorstown walking through Abergwynfi railway tunnel, which was closed to traffic on Sundays, to visit him at his home. They referred to him as 'John the Cape' whereas in his village he was known as 'The Lion' because of his strength and fierce nature.

The Rhondda was well supplied with chapels and public houses. In his first years in Tylorstown my father frequented both and he had many tales to tell about what went on in them. His sister-in-law, who was Irish, became cook in the Tylors Hotel, so he called there regularly to meet his brother, Harries. The miners came there from work to collect their wages from the miner who was in charge of a district. He would be paid their wages at the colliery office and would then personally distribute the money at the public house of his choice. At one period, wages were very good for some miners if they worked in a good district. My father would maintain that the tills of the Tylors Hotel on Friday and Saturday were too small to hold the sovereigns that the miners parted with. Even extra bowls would be overflowing in the last hours of serving, so that the gold coins were heaped in a small pile on the counter. There was such a rush for beer that not one of the staff could be spared to put the coins in the safe. By Saturday closing time tempers would have frayed to such an extent that brawls and fights would be started over trivial arguments which were subsequently settled on the mountain on Sunday morning.

The horse and cab had disappeared from Rhondda roads by the time I was born, but the stables were still in good order.

The Fever Hospital in Llwynypia had a dark-windowed box-like cab. It was brought to our house once, a complete surprise for me, and Ivor was carried out in a shawl-like blanket by a rather shabby top-hatted driver. Even the horse looked sad and shabby. My poor brother was taken away to the Fever Hospital and, as he went, he could just be made out behind the dark windows, waving bravely. He did not seem to be very ill but had to be isolated. We visited him in the hospital and were allowed to see him behind a window where he stood with several other boys.

Few people had the opportunity or money to travel far from their locality and I remember my father saying that he didn't visit Cardiff, which was, after all, only twenty miles away, for sixteen years when the children were small. Occupied with long hours at work, awkward shifts, family responsibilities and a busy chapel life which included at least three weeknight meetings, he had little time or inclination to travel far from Tylorstown.

My memories include brass-helmeted firemen, postmen with flat-topped helmets similar to those worn by soldiers in the Victorian era, and Breton onion sellers carrying strings of onions that hung on long poles which were balanced on one shoulder. Although cabs had gone, the tradesman's horse and cart remained. I pitied the tradesmen selling their wares in heavy downpours which seemed never-ending.

Injured miners would sometimes be carried on stretchers through our street. Children would stop playing their games and stare at the black-faced figure covered with a red blanket. He would have received First Aid, and in those days that was all he could expect.

From my bay window I loved to watch long, misty sheets of rain which extended from the floor of the valley right up to the low clouds which swirled their way on the upper mountain slopes. On such days, the dry beds of mountain streams which had lost their water through subsidence caused by mining, would become rushing torrents of cascading water which tumbled into the dirty river. Sometimes an urge would come over me to join the wild wet madness of the elements, so, well-buttoned and well-shod in black wellingtons, I would walk in the rain and stand in deep, clean puddles. I would return to the cosiness of my home freshened by the wind and rain.

Fortune-telling, peg-selling gipsy women sometimes knocked on our door, startling us when we confronted them on the doorstep. They never went away empty-handed; my mother bought their pegs to be rid of them quickly. I was fascinated when I first saw a gipsy woman. It was I who had answered the knock on our door, and the black, shining, piercing eyes, the nut-brown skin, the harsh voice and the beautifully coloured clothes were a novel sight.

Although my father did not partake in mountain-fighting, he was impressed by the courage and physical strength of fighting men who fought each other with bare-fisted ferocity. Blood flowed freely, and the contestants, stripped to the waist, fought until one of them was senseless on the grass or cut about so badly that he could not carry on.

The police were burly and were aware of these goings on, but diplomatically approached slowly and steadfastly to give the fighters and spectators time to disperse. This was important on Saturday night when the majority had been drinking strong beer. Invariably the fight would have stopped by the time the policeman had arrived, but his burliness and skill in handling a troublesome miner would be tested many a Saturday night. The 'mountain fighters' of Rhondda were renowned. If two men had a bitter argument which they could not settle, each would pay a mountain fighter to settle the dispute for them on Sunday morning. The gamblers would be busy 'backing the winner', which was very much against the good order of society, so the posted lookouts would warn of the approach of a policeman. The warning shout 'Bobby!' would put an end to the excited activity. For some poor fighter who was being battered by his antagonist, it must have been a welcome cry.

The godly were packed tightly in their chapel pews when this tough contest was taking place. I knew some of the mountain fighters when they had grown old. Some had been converted into sober, chapel deacons in the religious revival of 1904. Others were still rough and tough, and their sons fought in the fair which came to Tylorstown once or twice a year. Two immortal champion boxers from Rhondda thrilled the nation with their exploits. One was Jimmy Wilde who was called 'The Tylorstown Terror', and the other was Tommy Farr from Tonypandy. To the dismay of the more devout, Jimmy Wilde built a cinema in Tylorstown which soon became popular entertainment for the majority. The silent movies had short subtitles which could not be read by some of the older generation, either because they were shortsighted or because they could not read, and younger members of the family who accompanied them would read the captions aloud, but nobody objected. The Coliseum reeked with cigarette smoke even during Saturday afternoon matinees when only children were admitted, and we would come home for tea smelling like veteran smokers. My mother, although particular, never complained about my reeking clothes. She never became a cinema-goer, and I am almost certain she only went once to the cinema, and that was in Pontypridd to see *Ben Hur*.

I spent many long hours of my very early childhood in pointless, disciplined, chapel boredom, listening to long sermons and endless extemporary prayers in difficult Welsh, which was my second language. Later generations of children were taken to chapel as I was, but were allowed by their parents to take a book to read, or even to study a school text-book. I had to sit there patiently, but took more interest towards the end of the sermon when the preacher clearly indicated that he was approaching the conclusion. One sign he gave was closing the big black Bible, but I learnt to be patient and not be over-optimistic at this if his thumb was still between the pages. The Bible would be reopened and there could be another ten minutes of the sermon left to deliver. A few ministers taxed my patience by repeating this opening and closing of the Bible as many as three times. The last few minutes of the sermon fascinated me. There would be a wild, emotional outburst from the pulpit, which was encouraged by some of the deacons in the 'big seat' with shouts and noises of approval. The Welsh *hwyl* now gripped the congregation, and sitting next to my very emotional mother, I felt uneasy. The singing of the closing hymn was an opportunity for the congregation to give voice to its pent-up religious experience. It was Welsh hymn singing at its very best, rendered by Christians who sang from their hearts.

The social life of Tylorstown was satisfying. Like other South Wales

Hermon Chapel, Pont-y-gwaith.

mining villages there was no lack of skilled committee men who were happy to spend many hours a week in rooms hazy with tobacco smoke. Most of these men were on many committees which embraced the political, religious, cultural and sporting life of the village. Everyone I knew belonged to a religious or secular organisation and contributed in some way to the richness of the community. The committee men were the leaders and the rest were supporters.

There were two main divisions in Tylorstown. The head of the family determined the interests of his family by either attending chapel or frequenting clubs and public houses. Those who were church members had a broader outlook and could enjoy the church and the tavern. The chapel deacon would not race pigeons or greyhounds. The Nonconformist minister thundered that one could not be a hero in chapel and a hero at the bar of a public house, but the vicar who lived near me was a member in the clubs that were opposite his church.

Because unemployment continued, boys and girls became paler and thinner and shabbier in patched or ragged clothes. Boots were soon worn out by active boys, so it was a common sight to see some boys arrive in school on rainy days with the soles of their boots kept in place with string. Their long stockings would be soaked and their feet cold and wet, and the teacher would hang the stockings on the classroom fireguard before the blazing open fire or stove. For an hour or two they would be barefooted. Sometimes big boys would dump a pile of new shiny boots on the classroom floor. These had been sent to Rhondda by kindly charities. On one occasion there were spare boots and I was delighted to receive a pair.

Because my father was not unemployed, I did not qualify to attend the soup kitchen at dinner time. (In Tylorstown, chapel vestries were used as kitchens.) I felt hard done by because I could not join my friends who set off at the end of morning school with enamel utensils. I decided to join them on one occasion but was disappointed when I saw the queue of hungry children of all ages lined up before huge steaming cauldrons of soup where clean-aproned women ladled it out. Some children were desperately hungry because this was the only proper meal they were having throughout the miners' strike.

I was old enough in 1926 to realise that there was a miners' strike, but further than that, I had no idea what was going on. At that time, not one of the Rhondda coal mines had been closed and the people of Tylorstown were totally dependent, directly or indirectly, on coal-mining. Extra police were drafted into the area to keep order and enforce the law, and there was the inevitable clash with the miners because one of their members in Tylorstown decided to defy the strike call. Some streets had more hot-heads than others and many house-holders were unfortunate to have their windows smashed when riotous miners defied the police. Some local strike leaders served prison sentences for minor offences so that their followers would be deterred from causing trouble. Apart from the railway, there was little public or private transport, and the newspapers were the only media—and these were not sympathetic towards the miners' struggle. Consequently, despite the marches to focal points such as the De Winton Field in Tonypandy, the fighting miners were confined to their own villages. Even so, the strike lasted throughout the summer months.

I remember it being said that the Glamorgan Constabulary was the best-looking police force in Britain. Despite the bitter clashes, many Tylorstown people were soon saying with grudging pride that Glamorgan police were bigger, more smartly drilled and uniformed than those drafted into the valley from other parts of the country. Perhaps without justification, Maerdy, which is the last village in the Rhondda Fach, was singled out to be called 'Little Moscow'. There were many other mining villages equally abrasive to established authority and with as many Communists. In my life, politics and religion were closely inter-twined, so I was nurtured on a mixture of Christianity (which was very sectarian), Socialism and Communism.

The prolonged sunny weather during the 1926 Strike resulted in the formation of jazz bands which were lavishly costumed and drilled to parade-ground perfection. There were at least six jazz bands in Tylorstown and they gave a light relief from political argument and social strife. The long Depression which came in the thirties and lasted until the outbreak of war in 1939 undermined the personalities of the unemployed. The community was alert to the danger and societies were formed to combat frustration. It was a one-class society and human distinctions were measured by ability and personality rather than by rank and fortune.

I became very aware and annoyed at the problems and injustices that existed in Tylorstown. I naturally favoured the remedies put forward by the preachers. One of my favourite captions from a poster outside a chapel read as follows:

If you want to put the world right—start with yourself.

Chapter 4

Tŷ-Newydd.

I was eleven years old when my grandfather, Robert Williams, died. He was seventy-five when I was born and was already past eighty years of age when I became really aware of him. In the short time that we were together, however, I became extremely fond of him so that when he died I was very upset. It was the first death I had known in the family, and it certainly brought home to me, at that early age, the awful finality of death. He had epitomised happy holidays, the romance of the sea and an escape from everything I found unpleasant. I shall always remember him wearing a dark blue fisherman's jersey, and, come summer, come winter, he was always clad in his Welsh flannel shirt and underwear. He and dozens of others looked 'old salts' and they represented the last of the old-timers who served under sail. When they passed out of our lives, much of the romance of sea-port villages went with them.

He was born in 1844, and in the 1851 census, when he was six years of age, he was living at Penaber, Criccieth, North Wales. His father was William Williams, a successful farmer and landowner who was also a cattle dealer and a part-time drover. My grandfather remembered him fitting shoes on cattle before driving them to the English cattle markets. He must have been prosperous because, soon after 1851, the family moved to a fine house called 'Tŷ Newydd' in Llanystumdwy. At that time my grandfather was seven years of age. In 1876, when he was thirty-two years of age and had been married for four years, an artist came to paint a water-colour of the house. Fortunately I have a print of the original. To have such a splendid house with extensive grounds and a fast-flowing river with good fishing on the estate confirms the fact that William Williams was a man of means. His brother was the village blacksmith who, before the development of railways, was kept busy shoeing cattle for the drovers. During my grandfather's time, the drovers had almost completely disappeared from the Welsh scene and his uncle depended on shoeing horses for a living. The village boys habitually gathered near the busy smithy. One boy who came to see the horses being shod was David Lloyd George, who was destined to become famous as a statesman. Robert Williams, my grandfather, was a staunch Liberal and later became an admirer of David Lloyd George. He would have been delighted to hear that it was that great Welshman who later bought his father's home. The old statesman had declined the invitation to take heavy ministerial responsibility, and lived in Tŷ Newydd during World War II. Whilst there, he was honoured by being made Earl Lloyd-George of Dwyfor. His last years were spent in declining health and he died in the peace of the Welsh countryside where he had been born and bred.

To return to my memories of New Quay, one important part of my grandfather's house there was a large cellar which he rarely visited in his old age. It could be entered both from within and from outside the house. It was much easier to go through the black stable-like door from the outside than to venture down the dark, narrow stone steps from the end of the hallway. Normally only the upper half of the black door was open so that I was unable to rummage through the collection of boat equipment and bits and pieces collected throughout a lifetime spent seafaring. Old sails, coiled ropes, spare oars, an anchor, rowlocks, fishing net and lines, ship's lantern, oil-skins and a sou'wester, sea-boots and, in the centre, a clear space, a wooden covering over the well. The waters of the well were dark and cold, and inquisitive children could easily stumble into it—for that reason the lower half of the door was always bolted. A man delivering coal fell into the well which had been carelessly left uncovered and he was so frightened by the experience that he scampered away before receiving payment!

The well-water was only used for scrubbing floors and washing clothes. Drinking water was collected in cans from a pump at the end of the street. There was a splendid view of Cardigan Bay and the back of the pier from this pump, and down below at the bottom of the cliff there was a rocky beach known as Traeth-y-dolau. A few dozen cottages had their water-supply from this pump and it was a fine place to gather and gossip in summer weather. Water was rarely fetched on Sunday, for Saturday afternoon and evening were spent in preparation for the traditional Sabbath day of rest. (My grandfather did break the rule by cutting his cabbage on Sunday morning—so that it would be fresh for Sunday dinner!) Pumps and springs were in use at strategic places throughout the village. Spring-water was considered better than pump-water, and certainly I rarely passed the *pistyll* or spring by the old Co-operative stores without cupping my hands to have a drink. On the hottest of days it was delightfully cool and refreshing. My summer shoes and socks would get wet as I stooped to drink from the piped spring. Black barrels collected rain-water from pipes which led to the slated roofs and this rain-water was reported to be exceptionally soft and excellent for washing clothes.

My grandfather being an 'old salt', his grandsons knew that the best way to please him was to prove their competence in seamanship. Despite the hard life he had led on sea in all kinds of weather and in

New Quay Harbour.

very poor living-conditions on board the sailing-ships, he had remained jovial and I found him kindly. Although he was a competitive type, his sporting activities were confined to racing his boat in the annual regatta. He was probably as aware of what went on in a Spanish bullfight as in a cricket match. Being away at sea for most of his life, he had little interest in sport and, having been born in 1844, sport was not a big factor in Welsh life in his youth.

He had disappointed his parents because he did not settle down to study and took no interest in farming. Instead, he went to sea with his uncle who had a schooner which traded from Porthmadog. The furthest voyages they would undertake would be to continental ports. His first work on the boat, which had a crew of two in addition to his uncle, was to act as cook. So, it was in-between working in the galley, preparing the meals, and washing the dirty dishes and utensils that he learnt seamanship. He fancied himself as a cook but I found his dinners gross after my mother's cooking. Yet he never rebuked me if I failed to clear my plate, though I felt he was disappointed that my appetite was poor.

He had probably started his seafaring life before 1860. He was seventy years of age in 1914 when World War I started, and when the German U-boats began to sink our ships in large numbers with heavy loss of life he must have been thankful that he had never experienced war when he was a sailor. He had the worry, however, of having two sons and a son-in-law (all master-mariners) serving in the Merchant Navy throughout the war. I heard many men addressing him as Captain Williams, so I naturally assumed that he had passed the necessary examination. The title, however, was one of respect for the old man, an 'old salt' who had served the New Quay lifeboat for many years and had two sons who were captains. (The earlier captains had no paper qualifications, but after 1850 it was necessary to pass examinations to command a vessel.)

Although towards the end of his life, my grandfather was confined to his house, many old friends called regularly to see him. One was a retired police inspector and another, who lived next door, was Evan Williams who commanded the *Alpha*, a smart Fishing Protection launch which was anchored and tied to the pier. Evan was a huge man, but gentle and genial. However, when asked about his work on the *Alpha*, one would detect a hard glint in his eyes and another picture of Evan Williams emerged—a picture of the disciplinarian who was capable of defending himself and of handing out punishment when ruffled. The old men would make a great fuss of me when they visited my grandfather in his so-called cabin, which was was only large

Fishing boats at Cardiganshire beach.

enough for an old-fashioned Welsh settle and a tiny table and some chairs. I sometimes wondered how they managed to find room in that crowded little cabin where the assembly took place. In their time they had weathered terrible storms, and an evening together at my grandfather's provided an opportunity to ponder upon such adventures and exchange reminiscences.

There was a culm fire in this little room. Culm, or 'cwlwm' as my grandfather called it, was a mixture of clay and anthracite dust. It had been one of the main imports when New Quay was a port. Every evening he and I would settle quietly in the cabin after he had built the fire for the night with pieces of culm which he had shaped to the size of golf-balls. The whole operation, from the slow, hesitating, foot-dragging struggle to bring the dampened bucket of culm to the cabin, the thorough mixing with a trowel, the shaping of the pieces and placing them carefully in the grate and taking the bucket back, would take fifteen minutes or more. I watched my grandfather closely as he struggled to tend his fire. He boasted that it had not been out for years. Night and day, summer and winter, year after year, he had poked gently at the top of the dry, cake-like culm when he came into the cabin after a night's sleep, and a blue flame would shoot out. Within minutes the fire would be burning brightly ready to receive the kettle, so that he could make early-morning tea.

My grandfather met my grandmother in a sweet shop in New Quay, one of the many shops of this kind where home-made sweets, cakes and various odds and ends were sold. The coming and going of ships in the harbour made business worthwhile because the small profit was needed to augment meagre incomes. My grandmother spent much of her spare time in the shop, with her friend, whose mother kept it. Soon after they met in New Quay they were married, and settled in the village for the remainder of their lives, dying of old age within a few months of each other. If my grandfather ever yearned for North Wales, he could, on a clear day, see the summit of Snowdon from the end of New Quay pier, and he would sometimes return to his native Criccieth on visits. My mother remembers him, on one such occasion, arriving very late one night because he had walked some miles from where he had been given a lift from the railway station. He had taken a short-cut across fields, but unfortunately suffered for his trespassing and was chased by a bull. He had to run for his life to the beach, and, as the tide was in, he had to wade some distance before he knew it would be safe to resume his way across the fields. My mother remembers that the family came downstairs to greet and comfort him after his disturbing encounter with the fiercest of bovines!

Each year my summer holidays in New Quay brought new enjoyments. One year, I spent many days sitting beside a butcher in the driving-seat of his grey, box-like cart whose doors had perforated metal windows which allowed fresh air and dust to settle on the joints of meat—but succeeded in keeping out flies and other insects. At the end of his round he would leave the horse and cart on the main road near the sharp bend where the Blue Bell is located. He would later emerge far less sure-footed and climb laboriously into the driving-seat to clutch the reins lightly in both hands—a sufficient indication for the horse to start plodding homewards. The person who now returned home was a sad drooping figure, so different from the alert red-faced man I had met in the morning. His clear blue eyes had become glazed and even the brown hairs of his luxurious moustache hung limply from his upper lip.

I also had rides with the milkman who was younger and wilder than the butcher. He was a farmer and again, at the end of the delivery, would also make for the same sort of destination, in this case the Penrhiwllan Arms. One day I was told to drive the horse and cart to the farm whilst the owner enjoyed himself in the tavern. The horse went wild as we entered the country lane which was just a little wider than the cart; tugging the reins and shouting had no effect, and the shining milk-churn swayed from side to side. We dashed across the main road which was quiet in those days. I knew that the New Quay bus coming from the country would not be due to pass for some time and this knowledge made me feel better. The cart clattered, bumped and swayed like a Roman chariot as the horse galloped madly across the main road to New Quay, and fortunately for me there was no vehicle or pedestrian in sight. We came to a bend in the lane and a final dash ended the headlong gallop, as abruptly as it had started. Black and white sheepdogs, lying in the otherwise deserted farm yard where we had stopped, took little interest in us and the horse stood, quietly waiting to be released from the shafts. The escapade was not enjoyable and I was further saddened because I would be returning to Tylors-town the following morning. In any case I had made up my mind that I would not help the milkman again. The pretty maid in the Glyn would never have the opportunity again to scold me for spilling drops of milk on the dark blue stone doorstep. They had dripped from the full ladle as I filled the jug. The drops dried and spread into dirty blotches and she would have to wash the doorstep again! I would blush and apologise in slow, hesitating Rhondda Welsh, but she was relentless and took advantage of my good manners which she mistook for weakness, and her voice became harder and her Welsh more rapid. Her eyes flashed with disdain and momentary hatred. I would look up at her in fear thinking that she looked even more attractive now that her pent-up emotions were let loose—I would willingly have washed the doorstep for her! But the milkman would call me back to the cart and I would leave her standing in the doorway of the Glyn with its gleaming brass knocker, letter-box and weather-strip set in good oak.

In great contrast to this prim girl, I knew a farm girl who cared little how she dressed. She wore a long smock and battered hat and squelched through wet mud in wooden clogs (an essential for walking along the muddy roads), shouting hoarsely at the slow-moving cows on their way to be milked. She thwacked them gently if they were way-ward and when I heard her call the animals I felt as if I was being taken back to distant times.

My imagination had been kindled by the books I had read and by the stories I had heard, and I found plenty of reminders in New Quay to

Trading vessels at Llangrannog.

satisfy my boyhood dreams of the past. The old warehouse and sailing-loft had not been radically changed and put to other uses. The salt-house was the same as when my grandmother, and her mother before her, had gone to bag salt which was kept in a loft reached by climbing a narrow stairway. The Blue Bell, Wellington and Dolau were also unchanged from past years, when sailors from schooners and fisher-men from black herring-boats called there. They were lit by oil-lamps and new fangled gas-lamps, and in some of them beer was poured from the barrel into jugs. The kitchen and living quarters were very much part of these inns.

The lifeboat was manned, as was the coastguard station. The breeches buoy and rocket equipment were kept in an immaculate blue box on wheels which had a long T-shaped shaft, presumably for manhandling purposes. The harbour-master once sent me scurrying to his little house to fetch the log-book so that visiting Trinity House Officers could sign it. They had been rowed from their steamer by a dozen bluejackets who waited with upright oars for the business to be completed. I had run off without knowing what the excitable red-faced harbour-master had said in Welsh, and asked his wife for the keys of the lighthouse which hadn't been used for years. She refused, and I came back empty-handed, but an older New Quay boy soon put everything right and calmed the fuming harbour-master by sprinting the length of the pier and returning with the log-book.

The barque *Prince Llewelyn* of 256 tons was built in Cei Bach in 1859 and registered in New Quay the following year. She was seen by my great-aunt one fine morning from her bedroom window, in full sail, becalmed and waiting for a wind so that she could commence her long voyage which would perhaps take her round Cape Horn. She was a wonderful, never-to-be-forgotten sight. She was becalmed for several days and was a topic for conversation due to the whiteness and delicacy of her full-spread sails against the clear blue sea and sky—it was a view that could have been taken from a painting by a skilled artist. The last information I have of the *Prince Llewelyn* is that she foundered off St. Thomas Island in 1883.

The sea appealed to me, and the rhythmic sound of waves breaking over the pebbles of Traeth-y-dolau, followed by the rush of water hastening to return, helped to lull me to sleep. My grandmother, now forced to sleep alone because of my grandfather's infirmity, soon

New Quay schooner.

60

followed me upstairs and her head and shoulders would be silhouetted against the landing wall by the light of her tiny lamp as she made her way slowly, step by step, towards her bedroom.

I saw New Quay through the eyes of a small boy for the rest of my life. Future visits disappointed me because I failed to recapture the magic of boyhood—and the community was changing. I no longer felt that I was stepping back a little in time and that the people living in New Quay formed a Welsh community. From my elders I had heard of fairy-tale characters, such as Siani Pob Man who lived in a thatched cottage on the beach at Cei Bach. The cottage had been destroyed by the advance of sea and sand, and all that was left in my boyhood was a small pile of stones peeping out of the sands, showing where Siani had lived. Apparently, her home was flooded every high tide, so she would instinctively move with her chickens towards the back of the cottage where the floor was higher than in the front. Then there was Mari Pinch who pinched children who were restless during the chapel services. Needless to say, both these ladies were teased by high-spirited boys and Siani would throw stones at them if they came too near her cottage.

I used to visit Aberaeron to stay with people who had moved back there from the Rhondda. The husband did various jobs for the local council, one of which was to winch a cable-car with passengers across the harbour. His wife saw to it that he gave me a ride across the water, although officially the service had closed down for the night.

Probably the most spectacular shipwreck that took place in New Quay was that of the sailing-ship *Bronwen*. She was driven ashore at Pencraig, at the end of Rock Street on September 21st, 1891 and was so dangerously wedged on the rocks that New Quay lifeboat could not get near enough to rescue the crew. Their rescue had to be carried out by the coastguard whose equipment was pulled and pushed through Rock Street to the beach where, years before, stones for the pier had been quarried. Lines were fired by rocket and landed on the deck of the doomed vessel where figures were seen to be clinging desperately to the rigging. I was told that the captain, his wife and young son and the crew were brought to the safety of the beach by breeches-buoy where a crowd of villagers had gathered in gale-force wind and lashing rain. The *Pembrokeshire Herald* of 25th September 1891 states however that "the rocket brigade arrived, but were not required, the men climbing ashore along ropes communicating with the shore". There is no mention of the use of a breeches buoy. In *Reardon Smith 1905-1980* P. R. Heaton states that the first women saved by means of a breeches buoy were from the stricken *City of Cardiff* which was wrecked at Land's End in March 1912. The rescued women were the captain's wife and William Reardon Smith's niece.

The following stories were related to me as I sat quietly near the culm fire.

In World War I a sailing vessel was becalmed off Pencraig and refused to identify herself to the coastguards who saw her at first light. The Royal Navy headquarters at Milford Haven were informed and a warship was soon on its way. When the vessel was boarded, she was found to be German and was being used as a supply ship for their submarines which were active in the Irish Sea.

Excitement gripped the people of New Quay when a boatload of British survivors from a torpedoed ship landed on Traeth Gwyn. On another occasion it was sad to find a boat without oars, bearing a dead sailor scantily clothed and without identification, being washed onto the beach. He was buried in New Quay churchyard and the inscription on the gravestone reads 'Unknown Sailor'.

A German submarine commander in the First World War described the beach at Cwmtudu, which is between New Quay and Llangrannog, and gave a graphic account of surfacing his submarine when conditions were suitable, so that his crew could relax and 'stretch their legs' there. Today, this stretch of coast is of strategic importance because of the Ministry of Defence camp at Aberporth.

It is little wonder that as a result of family tradition, I soon made up my mind to become a sailor and follow in the footsteps of my brothers who had left home as soon as their parents allowed them, so as to join ships captained by their uncles. If I had gone to sea, I would have started differently. My uncles had retired and the Second World War was about to begin. The sea has remained a fascination, but surprisingly, I didn't even become a part-time sailor.

Recently I was reminded of the involvement of most New Quay families with the sea right up to my adolescent days when I read the biography of a Llangrannog sea captain who started his sea career with my uncle Capt. D. R. Williams on the SS *Ravenshoe*. My aunt would join her husband when the ship docked in Western European or United Kingdom ports, but before leaving New Quay she would call on the crew's families in the village to see if they had any special news for their men. She would collect their letters and hand them out when she arrived on board. When the ship was in distant waters and the voyage was particularly long, she would keep the families informed if she had any special news about the ship.

Chapter 5

I was nurtured in a religious atmosphere owing to my mother's experiences in the Revival of 1904-05 which was the last of a series of religious upsurges which swept across most of Wales, the first being the Methodist Revival of the late eighteenth century. To the very end of her life my mother retained her enthusiasm and simple faith, so that she became a leading figure in the religious life of Tylorstown.

There were others who had been young fiery evangelists and had left Christianity and chapel loyalty for Marxism. As a sixteen year old boy, Arthur Horner had walked through the night from Merthyr Tydfil to Tonypandy to witness the Tonypandy riots in 1910. There was great agitation leading to industrial strife for a guaranteed minimum wage and hours of work. The Eight-hour Act was passed in 1908, and there was also a grievance over working in seams where it was difficult to extract sufficient coal to earn a living wage. In contrast to the Revivalists, these were demands by some men for a more militant centralized union to challenge the coal owners. Many of these men were later fighting in the great battles of the Western Front in the 1914-18 War. Those who came back to the Rhondda, to the strikes and long depression, were very cynical. I spent hours talking to some of them. They were very poor and not welcomed in many places, and certainly no colliery manager wanted them in his work-force. They were troublemakers with a 'chip on their shoulders'. I found them as visionary as the 'children of the 1904-05 Revival', and they tended to have the same kind of one-track conversation. Their houses and clothes were often shabby and some were not particular about their personal appearance—such, at least, was my childhood impression. They preached violence against authority of all kinds in Britain, but they failed to gain a large following. There was nothing 'Welsh' about their philosophy, although they were, in many instances, from Welsh families. Unlike my father, they were no longer influenced by the chapel minister and the colliery manager, but were at war with existing conditions and sought social upheaval as in Russia to put things right. They did, however, command a grudging respect from my family and my parents' friends, particularly if they served a prison sentence for their political behaviour. I knew from the hours I later spent in their company that they were genuine Communists, but they were 'not nice to

Ebenezer Welsh Congregational Chapel. Rev. Glyndwr Jones, Minister.

know' according to my family: the red banners and flaming torches were as foreign as Marx, Lenin, Trotsky and Engels, and in any case they were anti-Christ. I preferred chapel singing and chapel people; I married a chapel girl. Paradoxically, I listened in awe to Arthur Horner, Harry Pollit, and many local 'firebrands', who struggled in vain for the rest of their lives to achieve the defeat of capitalism in Britain.

Overshadowing the Depression was the growing threat of war with Germany. I listened, debated, exchanged opinions, moralised and prayed, but did not make myself ready to fight. I did not want to accept the inevitable, but the growing uncertainty of the immediate future was a burden which I shared with other young people. The dangers that war brought were experiences that I had only heard and read about and therefore they did not frighten me. I hated, and shunned, the prospect of doing anything with my future apart from joining the Merchant Service and, if I had been encouraged at home, I would have left school there and then. My headmaster was furious when I confided my intentions to him and asked me to consider his position if all his sixth form decided to leave. I felt very guilty and ungrateful, so I became the first to break the family tradition of not joining the Merchant Service. I stayed in school but was never satisfied with my decision, and the fascination and love of the sea remained. Mining, despite its dangers, appealed to some of my friends and their family history was as tied up with the industry as mine was with seafaring. My mother would have been very proud if her boys had become chapel ministers, but my brother Ivor loved his life as a sailor and was proud to command a large vessel. However, I can't say I took to teaching with like enthusiasm. My happiness came with my marriage to Mair, to whom I owe so much.

My mother was taken ill before I left for College in Carmarthen, and this meant that my father, who was on a long sea voyage, would have to stay at home to look after her. He was very sad to leave his ship and a secure job, but by doing so he escaped being drowned through enemy action in the War, which broke out during the ship's next voyage. The S.S. *Ruperra* was torpedoed at two minutes to midnight and sank within minutes, leaving only a few survivors. My father would have been on duty in the engine-room with absolutely no chance of escape. He was so upset to hear of the fate of the officers and men that at first he wished he had been there with them, but when he recovered from his sadness he realised how fortunate he had been. My father visited a survivor in Barry hospital—he might have been the only one. His survival story was amazing. He had tried to escape through the port-hole because his cabin door was jammed, but was held tight by his hips. The rush of sea water in the ship smashed the cabin door and forced him out of the porthole. His hips were badly injured, I'm sure, but he was saved because help was near.

It was still peacetime when I left home for college, and I felt terrible. I had no idea how I would cope away from home, where I had the run of the place. My mother was so active with her chapel duties that for most of the time I could come and go as I pleased. Public-school boys leave home at a tender age to attend preparatory schools, so that, by the time they enter university or the professions, home-sickness has been long forgotten. In my case, having attended the local grammar school, I was a little frightened and depressed, and felt very insecure when I left the warm protection of the Rhondda Valley for Trinity College, Carmarthen. I managed quite well, considering my reluctance to leave home for the somewhat Spartan discipline of college life at that time. It was, however, a good preparation for the even more drastic change in circumstances when, in my first year in college, I joined the Territorial Army. The students were encouraged to join by the College Principal, Dr. Parry, and we had two days to consider his advice before signing to join the Territorials. This gave us no time to consult our people at home. My mother was alone at home and was recovering from a nasty stroke, so I could not consult her, as I had no wish to cause her any worry. I deliberated and finally came to the conclusion that I was being swept along by the tide of events. Paradoxically my motives for not joining the Territorials were purely selfish, and my motive for joining was not to lose face with my fellow students. When my next letter revealed that I had joined the Territorials, my brother-in-law was annoyed that I had not been given some time to consult my family. He had been a student in Trinity College, Carmarthen, in 1923 and Dr. Parry had been his Principal—he knew him from those days as a forceful personality. The students had received the King's shilling, signed the necessary forms and were committed to serve their country as soldiers before they had had the time to confer with their parents.

Our patriotism was mentioned in the leading newspapers and the following week we were training on the college lawns. Six months earlier I had signed my name not to take up arms for my king and country! In both instances I had signed because I was influenced by 'men of the cloth'. Dr. Parry was a canon of St. David's Cathedral and later became Dean Parry. He preached every evening in the College chapel and was always dressed in clerical garb. I signed the pacifist form, on the other hand, in my chapel vestry in Tylorstown, my minister the Rev. Glyndwr Jones, being a talented young man who was one of the intellectuals of Welsh Nonconformity. Both men were genuine and even to this day I cannot make up my mind which one was right.

My great fear was of being different from my fellows and of being accused of cowardice. It does demand a great deal of courage to be a pacifist when the popular trend is to take up arms in defence of one's country. It also takes great courage and self-discipline to be a brave soldier. It is moving to hear of some colonels leading their men 'over the top' in the First World War as calmly as if they were starting out on a country walk, or of the sergeant-major holding the hand of a young terrified soldier as they advanced towards the enemy lines in a bayonet charge. I have always admired bravery in whatever form it is demonstrated.

I suppose I faced up to my ineptitudes as a soldier, and to the moral conflict, with a certain amount of courage, but my greatest strength of character was a strong desire to survive and an ability to take a fair amount of punishment. I was better in defence than in attack. My father's inherited stubbornness was to be in my favour, and his kindly disposition made me slow to anger. These attributes were to stand in my stead in the war years, but then those years were mostly spent in captivity. In violent action and hand-to-hand fighting I don't think I would have been moved to aggression quickly enough. On the other hand, the foolhardy and the quick-tempered don't last as long as the cool and even-tempered.

I was thus a soldier in my first year in college and was pitchforked from the hearth very harshly, but I soon developed a protective layer of partial insensitivity around my inner feelings which helped me to withstand the pressures of physical and psychological difficulties. Indeed, I became so detached that I often felt I was an observer of events rather than a participant. I became very healthy in body and, in the Territorial camp, mixed with a cross-section of people. I was bowled over by the completely new experience of army officers and the authority and privilege that they had. For a Rhondda Valley boy brought up on Nonconformity and influenced by Socialism and Communism, they were strange beings. In a similar way, Welsh boys from humble homes in rural and industrial Wales must have been awed by the manners and money of public-school boys. It was easier when I realised that the majority of Territorial officers were from similar backgrounds to myself and had adopted the mannerisms of regular officers. Most of my fellow students, in their turn, when commissioned, must have been equally awe-inspiring to the new recruit in his ill-fitting uniform.

The fortnight in Porthcawl with the Territorials was spent under canvas in Dan-y-graig, and fortunately the weather was glorious. One night, however, we were unfortunate to be flooded in a severe thunderstorm, and this was my first experience of great discomfort! Our bedding was soaked and I was handed a mug of beer. Stringy hop leaves were floating on the surface. This was my first taste of beer—and, needless to say, I disliked it!

The warmth and friendliness of the Rhondda village I had left with such misgivings, had, without my realisation, given me a hidden strength of character. Tylorstown people knew each other and were concerned when the young men began to be called to the armed forces.

I left home with misgivings.

I was leaving an area which would lose much of its community spirit in post-war years, and I am grateful that I knew Tylorstown before this happened.

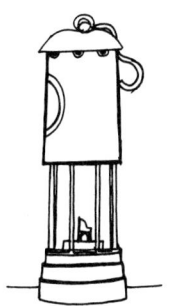

Chapter 6

"I came to the tall trees at the bottom of the street."

I returned home from the Territorial fortnight and marvelled at the comfort and attention I received at home. It was small wonder that I found life hard and robust at times in college and camp, but to be fair to myself, I was not alone in this. Alas for me, my refuge of snugness was very short-lived because the following morning my father handed me a telegram he had opened, informing me to report immediately back to camp. It was a mobilisation order. We had half-expected this to happen and took the news quietly. My brother was a chief officer on a B.P. tanker, so he was already in the front line if war broke out. Our main consideration was to keep calm for my mother's sake who had made a very good recovery. (My father had left the sea but would have been called back were it not for the fact that my mother was an invalid). I was pleased that I was being called up—and not my father. He was sorry that I had to go and told me some weeks later that he would go in my place if only he could! We were a very close family, prepared to shoulder each other's burdens.

Nothing untoward happened and I deliberately spoke very lightly about the problems and worries and my dislike of Army life. I realised that if either my brothers or I were injured in the War, it would seriously affect my mother's precarious health. However, she was to show amazing courage and faith throughout the War despite the fact that she had to face a really hard and testing time. When I came home on embarkation leave from Yorkshire and Durham I felt very sorry for her. I was now in the Royal Signals and had volunteered for foreign service in order to stay with a college friend, Vernon Minton, who was very upset when he was posted because his widowed mother, a country headmistress in North Wales, had already lost a son in an R.A.F. bombing raid in Benghazi, North Africa. His father, who was a schoolmaster, had died when the boys were quite young. Vernon often spoke of him. I was due to go on a course in Northern Command in York, but on impulse I told Vernon I would go with him abroad and take my chance.

There were many reasons why I had volunteered for the Territorials, and many reasons why I volunteered for Active Service—bravery and courage would have been at the bottom of the list! I went to wish my now frail, but pretty, mother goodbye, and my brother Ivor—the chief officer on the British Tankers—was shaving calmly in the next room. He was leaving later in the morning to join an Atlantic convoy! I had to tear my mother's hands from about my neck whilst my father—an old sea-dog by now—stood quietly waiting to accompany me to the railway station. It was sad, but what could we do? I looked back when I came to the tall trees at the bottom of the street—just for a last look—and my brother was watching me. We waved to each other and he turned into the house to console my mother who had to face the same ordeal again later that morning. I made up my mind to try and make light to my parents the unpleasant side of army life. My great regret was that I had not previously taken more interest in soldiering, and I felt very unprepared to face the future. I was a W.T. and a switchboard operator and had a premonition I was going to Singapore with Vernon. In a way, I was glad to get away from the humdrum life of moving from place to place in Britain and came to the conclusion that it would be better for me to see other countries. I did not want to be involved in fighting as some people say they are, but I was fed up with life in war-time Britain. I still felt that the Merchant Navy would have suited me better than the fighting Services.

Most of my school friends, who had some months to decide what they wanted to do in the War, joined the R.A.F. and became air crew and fighter pilots. Many of them were killed. Many became army or navy officers and others had responsibilities as warrant officers and N.C.O.'s. Although a number from my grammar school were killed, we fortunately lost few from my college year. One from North Wales was killed leading his men into action on the Normandy beaches.

The training, the open air and the good food prepared me physically for overseas. On reflection, I had been very fortunate in Britain to have been moved from places which had shortly afterwards been heavily bombed. The casualties had been heavy and I was very thankful that Fate seemed to have selected others. I wondered how long my luck would hold.

In the second winter of the War, I was stationed for a few weeks on the outskirts of Liverpool, so I took the opportunity to visit my New Quay grandfather's relatives. They had lost the Welshness which had characterised their forebears but there was a resemblance to my grand-father in some of them, particularly the white-haired old man who referred to him as Uncle Robert.

When darkness came, I told them that I had to return to my unit by eleven o'clock. They wanted me to stay until morning rather than travel across the blacked-out city which was being bombed practically every night. I could tell that they felt sorry for me because I looked so young and inexperienced, but I was reciprocally sorry for them because they were in great danger where they lived. Two of those present were Merchant Navy men waiting to return to sea for another perilous venture into the North Atlantic where submarines lurked. They walked with me to the end of the pitch-black street and gave me directions on how to get to Lime Street Station. The warning sirens sounded the alarm as I walked towards the station. Traffic stopped immediately so that there would be a clear way for rescue teams, fire-engines, ambulances and police. Searchlights probed the dark sky seeking out German planes that droned menacingly overhead and A.A. guns came to life. I was still a good distance from the railway station, and the last train would be due to leave. I continued walking on the tram lines which were in the middle of the traffic-free road and did not bother to wear my steel helmet. My only concern was that I might miss the last train. I noticed blue sparks bouncing off the neatly laid stones of the tramway and after a while realised to my horror that they were caused by falling shrapnel from the exploding A.A. shells. I ran for the shelter of a shop door, put on my steel helmet, and keeping close to the shelter of buildings proceeded on my way. The All Clear was sounded as I reached the station and I was on board the train as it left on time.

One of the grandest sights I can remember from Pembroke was the view of Milford Haven from the hill where the oil storage-tanks were. Below, on a fine summer morning, the deep blue waters of the Haven, stretching away to the open sea, would suddenly be disturbed by the white R.A.F. flying-boat preparing to take off on the routine Naval Air Command patrol of the Irish Sea and Western Approaches. The Sunderland flying-boat was the largest aircraft flown by the R.A.F.; it weighed 96 tons, and what a beautiful picture it made as it taxied down the Haven and gracefully rose into the blue sky. The son of old family friends, Squadron Leader Alan Blackwell, piloted one of these beautiful flying boats.

Another memory of Pembroke was doing 'flying picket' duties and sleeping on an historic warship *Warrior* which was the first ironclad. We slept in hammocks as the sailors had done in the mid-Victorian era and the crowded room where we spent the night had not been altered from the time the ship had been first fitted out. Another historic memory of the year I spent moving around England and Wales, was camping in Shugborough Park, the country seat of Lord Lichfield. Lord Gort, the commander of the ill-fated B.E.F., which was finally evacuated from Dunkirk, was staying in the beautiful mansion. Whilst there, I was on duty one Saturday evening when the password 'Cromwell' came through from the War Office—the signal that the German invasion of Britain had started. I passed the signal to the camp duty-officer and from there on we had a hectic time bringing officers and men back to camp. There was a stand-to in the carefully-prepared defence trenches. We would have been no match if German air-landings had taken place in Shugborough Park because we were less prepared, less experienced and poorly armed. The fighting would have been hard and spirited while it lasted.

Britain was bracing itself for the invasion. The general role in war-time Britain was 'carry on as usual', and this had been carried out so well in civilian life, that it was incredible that we were on the brink of disaster. The severe air-raids were to begin soon and the fortitude of the people was wonderful.

Most of Wales was regarded as a safe area and it was a great help that my parents were tucked away in the Rhondda, rather than in Cardiff, Swansea or any other great South Wales port. My mother seemed to have spent each summer in New Quay throughout the war years. The whole family was coping with the wartime pressures, each member in his own way.

Looking back, it is amazing how the unwilling mood of ordinary people in Britain to enter into a war with Germany was changed into a determination to defeat the Germans. This was largely achieved by the inspired leadership of Winston Churchill, who seemed to have been destined for this task. Strangely, the British people ousted him from the premiership as soon as the first elections were held, as if to emphasise that he had accomplished the task he had been destined for.

By volunteering for overseas service so as to remain with Vernon Minton, I had my name taken off a list for further training in York. I was tempting Fate by intervening in the normal flow of events in my life, and it resulted in my being captured by the Japanese. I was fortunate to survive the war. It was a moving experience when we marched past the saluting-base on our way to the troop train. We were aware that a number of us would not survive the dangers that were before us. The Royal Signals band played a stirring march and we had no thought of danger. Few who returned were sound in body or mind after their dreadful experiences. There was no escape from this consequence. Every move to the ship in Liverpool Docks went smoothly and the finality to me was when we walked from the troop train to the dock where the *Stirling Castle* was awaiting us. We went through the guarded gates and the red-capped military police were at every doorway inside the dock, as if to make sure that nobody made a dash for it! There were hundreds of service-men being tidily marshalled and everybody was accounted for. I felt trapped in a huge impersonal military machine where I was but a number. So much for the Nonconformist stress on the value of individuality which was applicable to my civilian life in a South Wales mining community. I felt much better on board ship and the tight supervision was no longer evident. I had been reminded of the stories I had been told by soldiers on the Western Front in World War I. Before an attack they were given a good stiff tot of rum, and when they went over the top they were covered by the Military Police who had orders to shoot those who turned back in fright.

The relaxed feeling on the troop ship suited me and I was quite happy on the trip out which took several weeks. When the ship drew away from the dock and an army band played patriotic tunes to stir the men from each of the four countries of the United Kingdom, 'Men of Harlech' was played for the men of Wales. Finally, as the ship left the dock, the band played 'Auld Lang Syne' and the troops cheered and whistled madly. As we headed for the open sea, the mountains of North Wales were to be clearly seen. A smart young soldier approached and ruefully commented that he lived at the foot of the distant mountains. He was fortunate to survive the war, and by chance I met him forty-three years later at his home in Bethesda. His experiences in the Far East had broken his health and he never fully recovered.

On the open sea I could not but think of my brother Ivor who was in constant peril. We slipped through the Irish Sea in the growing darkness and made for the Firth of Clyde through the night. The convoy was gathering here and I saw one of our escort submarines passing us a day before we sailed. Some of the pale-faced crew waved cheerfully as their sinister-looking craft silently glided past. I felt very sorry for them and they looked at us sympathetically. The cruiser *Glasgow* was controlling the convoy. Off we went into the grey-blue waters of the North Atlantic and made our way to Newfoundland; we sailed south, then recrossed the Atlantic to Freetown, zig-zagging all the way until we eventually reached Cape Town. We were fortunate on this trip. There was a submarine sighting and there was a Red Alert. Depth charges were hurled overboard and a plane from the *Glasgow* kept searching, then a large smudge of oil was reported and that was the end of that incident. Some miles from Cape Town, the *Glasgow* wished us goodbye and Godspeed, and returned northwards to British waters. The merchant ship *Caernarfon Castle*, which was termed an 'armed merchantman', took charge of us. H.M.S. *Glasgow* and the *Stirling Castle* survived the war but the *Caernarfon Castle* was lost in the South Atlantic after an encounter with a better-armed enemy ship. I was very fortunate in having a place on the 'A' deck of the *Stirling Castle* and I felt that if we had to abandon ship I had a good chance of survival. Those down below would have little chance in the rush to get on deck. I liked the sea where others hated and feared it, for I felt at home on board ship and it was even more obvious that I would have been much happier serving my country as a sailor. It was a very dangerous place to be in wartime, but that did not seem to worry me. I felt like a fish out of water in the army!

I was very thrilled to see Cape Town nestling at the foot of Table Mountain, exactly as I had seen it in my school Geography book. The seas were mountainous and I went out on the sloping decks to see the huge walls of green water that hid the sky. The 22,000 ton *Stirling Castle* wallowed like a toy ship in the gigantic rollers and the crazy angles made it difficult to stand on deck. The small red-faced chief officer who had a Punch-like nose walked with accustomed ease on his tour of inspection.

The snow-white wooden decks, which were hosed and scrubbed every morning, were wet with sea spray. I had taken my blankets and slept soundly on deck in warm calm weather. The moon and stars and the gentle throb of the engines and the creaking of wooden fixtures, would soon lull me to sleep. Near the Equator, the Plough and the Southern Cross were visible, each low on their respective horizons. For me there was little military discipline because I belonged to a small specialised unit. The infantry were constantly being trained by weapon instructors. They were a grim reminder that we were wartime soldiers.

Cape Town gave us a wonderful welcome. Scores of cars were awaiting us and Vernon and I had our fortunes told in one house. My future was good. She hesitated with Vernon. Although he would survive the War, he would die in middle age. I thought he was most fortunate to have survived the war, and he must have thought the same about myself because there were times when we were both at a very low ebb and looked dreadfully ill. On another occasion we were taken to the home of a lady doctor whose husband was Chaplain General to the South African forces. Her brother-in-law was Edgar Wallace, the famous writer of detective stories. She was horrified when we told her that we had been taken to have tea where the ladies told our fortune. She said it was listed as a place where information was gathered for German intelligence. Apparently, there was a strong pro-German element in South Africa and, had it not been for General Smuts, the South Africans would not have entered the combat to assist Britain. She was of British ancestry and was very much against Germany. Most Boers had not forgotten the Boer War and were waiting for the opportune time to settle old scores. A very attractive African girl with chocolate-brown skin served us with tea and I considered her lucky, being employed in such a nice house. The doctor, who was now smoking a long cigarette in a long holder, said that she only smoked once a day, and that was after the evening meal.

Another house we went to was a family house. There was a schoolboy there who was fond of rugby. On other days we went exploring Cape Town on our own and it struck me that there was almost a complete absence of black people in the streets which were signposted in English and Afrikaans. The Australian troops who were bound for the Middle East had been here before us and they had behaved wildly. They had far more money to spend than we had and they certainly made their presence felt. Vernon and I were very quiet and too over-awed by our experiences to be wild. Neither of us had learnt to drink much alcohol. Our only vice was smoking which was normal adult male behaviour in those days, so we were like 'innocents abroad'. We hadn't earned a 'penny piece' in civilian life and had lived on pocket-money. Anyway, we were managing to cope in the strange city. I visited the cemetery and saw my cousin Danny's name in the records of the sexton's office. Unfortunately the cemetery was closed that afternoon and the *Stirling Castle* was sailing in the next twenty-four hours. (There had been a sailing delay because of a German naval presence in the Indian Ocean). We were sailing for Singapore on our own and it was decided that for the trip to Bombay we would need protection. We had to await the arrival of a cruiser. Not one ship of the convoy that left the Firth of Clyde had been lost, but most were torpedoed later in the war.

Thousands of British troops called at Bombay, and although it was a very colourful city, I was shocked at the great poverty. Cape Town had been similar to a city like Cardiff in many ways, and the majority of the inhabitants I saw were of European stock. Bombay, however, was my first experience of seeing people of a different culture and colour and observing how they lived. The beggars were frantic in their efforts to obtain money from Vernon and me. They were filthy, and big flies hovered over their nauseating sores. I was aghast at such suffering, but little did I realise that my friends and I would be like them within a year. One screaming woman pushed her children against me, and thrust her baby close to my face. I would have given her help, but I had little money. If we had given to one we would have been overwhelmed with beggars of all ages. Our final shock came at nightfall when scores of people prepared their beds on the pavements. We looked on in disbelief and Vernon would not believe me when I said they were homeless. We were disgusted when two bullying red-capped military police came from nowhere and hit the driver of a horse and two-seated carriage with heavy clubs as we were bargaining for the price of a ride back to the *Stirling Castle*. More blows on his back and shoulders, and verbal insults, made him cringe and the 'red caps' politely ordered us to get in the carriage. Still more blows and threats of worse treatment sent us cantering away and, surprisingly soon, the lights of the *Stirling Castle* came to view as we rounded a corner. We were relieved to climb the gangway and escape from the heat and sordid poverty of Bombay.

When I saw the old fort at the entrance of Bombay harbour, I was reminded of school history text-books which traced the story of the East India Company. I had never thought that I would visit India as a soldier.

Uneasiness was making me unhappy as we left Bombay and headed for Singapore. The future was not inviting. The threat of war with Japan did not bother me so much as having to settle down to army routine. I had enjoyed my time on the *Stirling Castle*. I loved the sea. Many of my friends had shown great understanding and kindness and some had gone out of their way to encourage me to come to terms with the turn of events. The sea was in my blood and it has beckoned me all my life, but I have never responded. It is, I'm sure, a primitive call, and even now, in the latter part of my life, the sound and sight of the sea in all its moods gives me satisfaction which mountains and beautiful countryside cannot give.

The next few years were to be a stern time for those trapped in Malaya and Singapore. The defeat was swift and complete, and captivity meant a relentless struggle to survive Japanese cruelty, the ravages of disease, the filth, degradation and starvation. Those who survived can never forget these who perished in such circumstances. It is a very sad tale about suffering and war, and it will be the subject of my next volume.

Appendix 1

Summary of Establishment of Tylorstown Collieries

Although the first Rhondda coalmine was opened in **1812** by Walter Coffin, it was not until the Taff Vale Railway reached Ferndale and Maerdy in **1856** that Thomas Wayne started sinking a shaft in the area now known as Tylorstown. The site was known as "Pwll Waynes" (Wayne's Pit) or "Pont-y-gwaith Pit" which eventually became No. 8 Colliery. Thomas Wayne gave up the project because of continual strikes and disputes with the workmen.

In **1872** Alf Tyler, a London business man, bought the mineral rights of Penrhys Farm and two shafts were sunk which eventually became No. 6 and No. 7 Collieries. After a few difficult years of search, coal was eventually found in **1876**, and the first trucks of Tylorstown coal reached Cardiff in **1877**.

In **1888** D. Davies and Sons bought "Pwll Waynes".

In **1894** D. Davies and Sons bought Alf Tyler's collieries.

Finally, in **1901**, D. Davies and Sons opened No. 9 Colliery.

There were thus four collieries operating in Tylorstown alone, which gave employment to between five and six thousand men and boys.

D. Davies and Sons numbered the Tylorstown Collieries **6, 7, 8** and **9**. They were sold to the Powell Dyffryn Group and then nationalised in 1947.

Appendix 2

New Quay, Dyfed, Sea Captains in the same family

Jenkin Phillips 1750-1821
Phillip Jenkin Phillips 1773-1817
Jenkin Phillips 1825-1883
David Jones 1821-1869

First half of the Twentieth Century

Captain D. R. Williams, *Hafan Dawel*, New Quay.
Captain Ivor Williams, *Kenmare*, New Quay.
Captain Roy Jones, *Creiglan*, New Quay.
Captain Danny Jones, *Creiglan*, New Quay.
Captain Ivor Davies, Tylorstown, Rhondda.

There were others who were seafarers and in the wider family tree there were many more sea captains in New Quay.

Joseph Jones (see page 26), my great-great-great-great-grandfather, 1759-1839, was an Excise Officer in New Quay.